GOD IN MAN'S EXPERIENCE

GOD IN
MAN'S EXPERIENCE

The Activity of God in the Psalms

by

LEONARD GRIFFITH

HODDER AND STOUGHTON

Printed in Great Britain for Hodder and Stoughton Limited,
St. Paul's House, Warwick Lane, London, E.C.4,
by Lowe & Brydone (Printers) Ltd., London

DEDICATION

(Adapted from a prayer of Lancelot Andrewes)

To my parents wise and good,
my wife loving,
my children devoted,
my teachers patient,
my friends faithful,
my colleagues loyal,
my congregations longsuffering,

To the saints of all generations,
scholars,
scientists,
poets,
musicians,
preachers,
artists,
leaders,

To all who have helped me by their

writings,	sermons,
conversations,	silence,
gifts,	prayers,
laughter,	tears,
praises,	rebukes,
examples,	wrongs,

to all who have brought the living God into my experience

I gratefully dedicate this book

and give God the glory.

CONTENTS

ACKNOWLEDGEMENTS

The extract from *The Questing Spirit* edited by Halford E. Luccock and Frances Bretane is reprinted by permission of Coward-McCann of New York; "The Conquerors" by Harry Kemp, from *Masterpieces of Religious Verse* edited by James D. Morrison, is reprinted by permission of Harper and Row, Publishers; some of the scripture quotations, where their origin is not specified, are taken from the *Revised Standard Version of the Bible*, copyrighted 1946 and 1952.

INTRODUCTION

The Malaysian sitting next to me in the aeroplane could not contain his curiosity. He had boarded the plane at Singapore and was on his way to study English literature at the University in Hobart, Tasmania. I was travelling from London to Australia to fulfil a nine-week's engagement in several cities. As far as Singapore I had three seats to myself, so I tried to employ the long, tedious hours usefully. It was a golden opportunity to do some uninterrupted work, and I confess that, even after what seemed like the whole population of Malaysia crowded into the plane, I continued to work in anti-social silence. But the young student was fascinated. Out of the corner of his eye he had been watching me as I underlined words and phrases in a tiny book and scribbled notes on a tiny pad. At length he broke the silence and said politely, "Do you mind if I ask what you are doing?" "Not at all," I replied, "I am planning a book."

So that's where I began the serious preparation of this manuscript—over South-East Asia at thirty thousand feet up in the air. For a long time I had been wanting to write a book on the Old Testament Psalms but had been deterred mainly by the pressure of other duties and by the fear that I could draw no fresh insights from this familiar area of Scripture which for centuries has been the devotional heritage of the human race. I had often preached on isolated Psalms, but so had other preachers, and there seemed no reason to make my miscellaneous sermons the substance of a book unless a common theme of sufficient importance drew them together. At last I discovered that theme in my daily devotions.

It is true to say that I have lived with the Psalms and made their ideas and phrases so much a part of my own thought that I feel as though I know their authors as intimately as I know my family and friends. Not that I have ever been greatly concerned about the exact identity of the authors. It seems reasonable to go along with tradition and suppose that David, the shepherd and king, did in fact compose some of these hymns of ancient Israel. It is obvious that others were composed by different writers at different periods in Israel's history. But who bothers to consult the name of the author of a hymn before making it a means of worshipping God? How many worshippers today can actually tell you who wrote such familiar and beloved hymns as "O God, our help in ages past", or "Jesus, the very thought of thee"? The value of a hymn or poem lies not in its authorship but in the measure that it gets inside the soul of the reader and expresses the thoughts that he himself cannot find words to express. Undoubtedly each Psalm was written at some time by someone, but the Psalms themselves have survived because they are timeless and because they are the utterances of every man in the presence of God.

Actually this book has been in preparation for many years, because for many years I have begun my practice of early-morning devotions with a Psalm read aloud. It would be difficult to estimate how many times I have gone through the Old Testament Psalter in this way. The Psalms have helped me to pray. They have been my "Introit", my means of access to the presence of God. They seem to differ from other Scriptural writings in that they are more the inspired words of men than the inspired Word of God. Through the rest of the Bible God speaks to man, but through the Psalms man speaks to God. The Psalms show us how man ought to speak to God. No wonder they have been woven into the great liturgies of the Church. Where else does one find language that sets forth so sublimely the attributes of God as well as the moods of man in the presence of God. I marvel at the Psalmists—not only for their literary genius but for their boldness to approach God, to adore and praise God, to plead with him and get angry with him, to wrestle with him and throw themselves upon his mercy. Often, when I read a Psalm, I say to myself, "This is exactly how I feel. This is what I want to say to God. I *shall* say it to God"; and, having begun my prayer with the Psalmist's words, I then find courage to continue praying in my own words.

I keep a diary of my morning devotions. It includes my prayers for each day, my petitions for personal needs, my intercessions for other people, for the Church and for the institutions of society. The diary includes also a word or two to describe the character of God in each of the Psalms. One Psalm sets forth God's eternity, another his creatorhood or his sovereignty, his providence, justice, grace, mercy, love, etc. After a while I found myself writing beside certain Psalms, "*The God who . . .*", then a verb to describe some phase of God's activity particularly present in the experience of the author. For example, the writer of the 23rd Psalm found him to be a God who cares; the 51st—a God who pardons; the 139th—a God who pursues. It was then that the common theme came into view, and the idea gripped me of going carefully through the whole Psalter to study every phase of God's activity in the experience of the men who wrote the Psalms. I was doing this on the aeroplane, marking a tiny copy of the Psalter and scribbling in a tiny notebook, when the young Malaysian struck up a conversation. At the top of the notes I had written the title, "God in Man's Experience".

I felt sure, as I now feel doubly sure, that a book on this theme, if it inspires a new and deep study of the Psalms, will meet a genuine need. Today, as never before in our lifetime, people are muddled and confused in their thinking about God. Not many feel that they have the mental qualifications to say categorically that there is no God. They would not call themselves atheists but they do confess to being agnostics. They are not sure and they are too intellectually honest to pretend to be sure. They admit that God may be real enough for others, but he is not real for them, and very often they wish that he were real. We make a mistake if we restrict the agnostic spirit to the glib debunkers of religion who get more attention in the magazines and on television than they deserve. Agnosticism can be an agonizing frame of mind, as seen in modern plays and novels where characters cry passionately for some ultimate truth that will solve the senseless riddle of existence.

More recently and more frequently men have not been asking, "Is there a God?" they have been asking, "What is God like?" That question broke into the newspaper headlines when the Bishop of Woolwich, in his controversial *Honest to God*, made popular the thought of Paul Tillich who had been insisting that God is not a Being separate and distinct from the world; he is Being Itself, the ground and depth of all Being. The Bishop's book and its attendant publicity seemed to imply that we needed a new image of God; and he may have been right. We needed it to correct the too-remote concept of God as an impersonal Life Force and the too-chummy concept of God as "a celestial chore-boy loafing around his universe, pitifully pleading to be made use of". The acquisition of a new image of God, however, presupposes familiarity with the old image, and this surely takes too much for granted. It may be true that scientific man has difficulty finding a place in the scheme of things for the God of the Old Testament, but has scientific man come to terms with the God of the New Testament? This God has but one image—the character of Jesus Christ. "He is the image of the invisible God." The writer of the Fourth Gospel states the Christian position explicitly: "No one has ever seen God"; but, he adds, telling us all that we have ever known and all that we need to know, "the only Son, who is in the bosom of the Father, he has made him known."

Even staunch Christians, however, ask a more searching question about God. They concede that there is a God "in whom we live and move and have our being" and that he is like Jesus, but they want to know if he is a *living* God. They ask, "What has God done, what does he do and what, if anything, is he doing right now? Is he alive and active in his world?" The question becomes intensely personal as we contemplate the many factors in human life that give the world the appearance of an orphanage or a family no longer under parental control and care. There is a story of the devil briefing his minions. "What will you tell men?" he asks the first. "I shall tell them that there is no God." "No use. They won't believe you," the devil replies. "What will you tell men?" he asks the second. "I shall tell them that there is a God but that he doesn't love love them." "They won't believe that either," the devil replies. "What will you tell men?" he asks the third. "I will tell them that there is a God who loves them but that it needn't make any difference." "Fine," says the devil, "Off you go!"

That is the question that people ask about God. Granted that he exists and that he is like the loving Jesus, does it make any difference? Is God a real factor in life? Does he deal with us, and must we deal with him? Is he a Person who does things for us, and, if so, what exactly can we count on him to do? In every man's world there are persons whose existence deeply affects his own, because he lives under their authority and protection. A child obeys his parents who gave him life and who surround him with the love and security of home, he obeys his teachers who instruct him in knowledge, he obeys the policeman who guards his safety, he obeys the doctor who protects his health. These people are real characters in the drama of our lives, and we cannot ignore them because we need them, and there is no doubt what they can do for us. Is God also a member of the cast? Is he also a real, live character in the drama of life and, if so, how does he deal with us and what does he do for us?

The question can be answered only in terms of pesonal experience, and many of the Psalms answer it because they are written in the ink of personal experience. There are no speculative theologians among the Old Testament poets. They do not try to prove the existence of God, nor do they fashion finely-woven doctrines about the image of the Godhead. Any general propositions about God, which they exhort us to believe, derive entirely from their convictions about God as they experienced him. The Psalmists were men who consciously brought God into their experience and, in so doing, found that he did for them what no one else could do. He heartened them in their fears, supported them under their burdens, guarded them against danger, calmed them in their stress and unified their lives around his single, controlling purpose. God did all this for them and more besides, and it was in response to this activity of God that they wrote their Psalms.

The Psalms have meaning for us because they begin where we are. They find us in our human situation and they show us what happens when we bring the light of God to bear upon our human situation. Little wonder that people continue to treasure the Psalms as an aid to personal devotion. Little wonder that they find them a means of access to God. No collection of writings in all the world so completely covers the whole range of God's activity in man's experience. Every man can find himself somewhere in the Book of Psalms. There will be at least one Hebrew poet with whom he can identify himself, whose situation mirrors his own and who can therefore take him by the hand and lead him into the presence of God. The following chapters attempt to demonstrate that truth.

It will be evident in these pages that I make no claims to Biblical scholarship. The reader, who wants a detailed exegesis of each Psalm as well as a literary analysis and an exhaustive treatment of its authorship and historical background, will have to consult, as I have consulted, the experts in the field. What I attempt to offer are faithful expositions based less upon the study of commentaries than upon the use of the Psalms in my own practice of daily devotion. My major concern has been to relate the Psalms to real life and to show each Psalmist's experience as a link between our experience and God. Some of the shorter Psalms I have been able to expound verse by verse, others I have taken by stanzas, and in some cases I have attempted simply to develop the central theme. At all times I have set the Psalms in their total Biblical context, placing the Psalmists' experience of God in the light of God's complete revelation of himself in the life, death and resurrection of Jesus Christ.

Except where otherwise indicated, I have based these expositions on the *King James Version* of the Bible, not because I consider it to be more "inspired" but because it is more familiar and because it retains a poetic beauty that one does not always find in later translations. I have arranged my selections of Psalms in their Biblical order. It would have been possible to arrange them in a logical sequence of thought to correspond with the great doctrines of the Faith or the seasons of the Church Year, but this is something that the reader may want to do for himself.

Gratefully I acknowledge my debt to numerous commentaries and devotional aides. Because these chapters were preached as sermons, mostly to my congregation at Deer Park Church, Toronto, I acknowledge a debt to the regular worshippers who encourage and respond to Biblical preaching. I thank the two office secretaries at Deer Park, Miss Sandra Helm and Mrs. Ann van der Ree, who prepared the manuscript; and I thank Mr. Charles Reid, editor of the Deer Park Magazine, who read the proofs; I am especially grateful to Mr. Edward England, Religious Editor of Hodder and Stoughton, who gave assurance that a book on this theme would be welcomed and whose enthusiasm encouraged the task which began seriously on an aeroplane over South-East Asia.

A man cannot borrow another man's experience of God but he can be helped by another, as I have been helped by the men who wrote the Psalms. Now I want to share the overflow of my spiritual treasure. If this book encourages a single reader to open his life to the healing, renewing, empowering, redeeming activity of God, it will have accomplished its purpose.

A. LEONARD GRIFFITH

GOD HIDES

The author of a recent book makes this statement: "What interests me is not whether God exists but, assuming He exists, what He is like and what on earth He is up to at the present moment." That writer speaks for all of us. Most of us do not have to be convinced that there is a God of some kind, nor do we frankly care about what the theologians call "the right image of God". God can be above us, around us, within us or all three as long as he is somewhere. We are more concerned to ask the question, "What is God doing?" or more precisely, "Where has God gone?" The Creator and Ruler of the universe, call him a Supreme Being or Being Itself, is too often conspicuous by his absence. Sometimes this world seems such an undisciplined madhouse and our personal lives so utterly at the mercy of blind fate that we are tempted to echo the bitter complaint of H. G. Wells who said of God that "He is an ever-absent help in time of trouble".

The complaint is not new; it is as old as man's experience of God. All through the Bible you find men of integrity and faith asking the bewildered question, "Where has God gone?" The Bible is a record of God in man's experience. It shows us the activity of God in the life of man and the life of his world. God hears, God speaks, God guards and God rescues, but occasionally he does something else, something that seems strange, capricious and even cruel: *God hides*. So it must have seemed to Noah, floating about on his gigantic ark with nothing around him but empty waters and a sky that held no hope. So it must have seemed to the ancient Hebrews enslaved in Egypt for four centuries, their sufferings mocked by the unanswering silence of heaven. So it certainly seemed to the tortured Job who shook his fist at heaven and dared God to come out of hiding and face him like a man. From the years of exile came this anguished prayer of a prophet; "Truly, thou art a God who hidest thyself."

So the writer of the *10th Psalm* has plenty of company when he begins with a prayer of perplexity: "*Why standest thou afar off, O Lord? why hidest thou thyself in times of trouble?*" He never answers his own question, "Why does God hide?" but he does show us how different types of men react to the apparent absence of God. There is the perplexed moralist who simply cannot understand why the King should vacate his throne and leave his kingdom in complete chaos. There is the immoral materialist who cuts loose like a gangster, saying in his heart, "*God hath forgotten: he hideth his face; he will never see it.*" And there is the man of faith who stubbornly believes that "*The Lord is king for ever*" who will come out of hiding in his own time to punish the evildoer and vindicate his loyal subjects.

Yet we are still haunted by the question which the Psalmist asks but leaves unanswered: "Why standest thou afar off, O Lord? why hidest thou thyself in times of trouble?" That God is a God who hides there can be no doubt. Job speaks for every man in his plaintive cry, "Oh that I knew where I might find him! . . . Behold, I go forward, but he is not there; and backward, but I cannot perceive him . . ." There are times in our experience of God when he seems to remove himself from our sight like a parent who hides behind a tree in the park to play a joke on his unsuspecting child. But a loving parent shows himself when the child begins to cry, so why doesn't a loving God do the same thing? Why does he hide at all?

Is it possible that God purposely hides himself *so that we may rediscover him as he actually is?* These days we cannot help being perturbed by what amounts to a conspiracy of silence about God. We seem to have passed beyond the stage where slick journalists and television personalities proudly declare their disbelief in God. Now we have reached the point where all sorts and conditions of men regard God as a dead issue; they do not even bother to talk about him any more. We put this down to man's indifference, but Paul Tillich gives another view when he sees it not as man's doing but as the work of God himself. Tillich suggests that from time to time God actually reveals himself by creating silence about himself. In order to protect the sanctity of his Name he withholds from a generation what was natural to previous generations—the use of the word "God". Tillich asks, "Is the secular silence about God that we experience everywhere today perhaps God's way of forcing his

Church back to a sacred embarrassment when speaking of him?"[1]

The Church and Christian people have not always spoken about God with sacred embarrassment. Often we have spoken with a glib familiarity that almost borders on blasphemy. One recalls with horror those American popular songs which referred to God as "the regular Good Guy" and "the Man Upstairs" and one still staggers slightly at the glamorous film star who described God in her best bedroom voice as "a livin' doll". This is no worse than the popular debate about the so-called "image" of God which has titillated television viewers and provided copy for spiritually-bankrupt newspapers. After hearing his Name irreverently mouthed by people who have no serious intention of honouring it, God may indeed have created a silence about himself and withdrawn his Name from currency until people learn again to speak that sacred Name with reverence and godly fear.

Why does God hide? we ask, forgetting that the God of the Bible is a God who hides himself behind clouds and thick darkness. If God were always obvious, even to eyes which are clouded by unbelief and sin, he would not be God at all but an idol of our own devising. Jesus taught us to address God familiarly as "Our Father", but he added to that address the qualifying phrase, "who art in heaven", so that we might always be aware of the remoteness, the otherness and the transcendence of the God who allows us to experience him here on earth. Our God is a Being shrouded in mystery, an infinite Being beyond the scope of our finite minds, whose judgments are unsearchable and his way past finding out. His very hiddenness makes him God, and *that* is the truth we must relearn, the truth that makes us tremble even to take his Name upon our lips, if we are going to rediscover God as he actually is.

Is it possible that God purposely hides himslf *so that we shall look for him where he is actually to be found?* It could be that God is not hiding at all but that we are searching for him in the wrong places. Our trouble is that we expect to find God only in the lovely experiences of life. When we stand in a majestic mountain valley and watch the sun going down behind the snow-capped peaks in a blaze of glory, then we say that we feel

[1] Paul Tillich, *The Eternal Now* (S.C.M. Press, London, 1963), p. 84.

B

close to God. When our hopes are fulfilled and all our plans succeed, then we say that God has been very good to us. When we feel physically strong and know ourselves surrounded by human love and laughter, then we say that we are face to face with God.

But that was not the experience of the men who wrote the Bible. They were realists. They looked for God in beauty, success and happiness, but they also expected to find him in ugliness, failure and sorrow. They saw God not only in the sunshine but in the storm, not only in the flower but in the earthquake, not only in plenty but in famine, not only in health but in sickness, not only in victory but in defeat. They recognized God in life's sterner as well as its pleasanter aspects; and they saw his relationship with them not in terms of comfort but in terms of power.

"Why standest thou afar off, O Lord? why hidest thou thyself in times of trouble?" This point of view supposes that God has nothing to do with trouble. It is the point of view of many who look out today on the world's hunger and suffering and violence and ask indignantly, "Where has God gone? Why doesn't he put in an appearance and do something about it all?" But surely this betrays a mistaken idea of God. It supposes that God is an external factor whom we can bring to bear from the outside on our troubles if we pray to him hard enough. The Bible teaches that God is an internal factor always at work within our human affairs and that many of our troubles are the result of our refusal to recognize him and work along with his purpose. It is not always God who hides from us but more often we who hide from God. We might discover that truth if we stopped telling God what he ought to do and tried to co-operate with him in what he has already done and is doing now.

One dark night on a deserted beach off the south coast of Wales a lonely man prepared to commit suicide. He looked back over a chequered career which had begun in a God-fearing Welsh home and had taken him into the Christian ministry and thence to journalism and every shade of religious and political belief, ending in anarchy and atheism, and he saw it all as a long succession of dismal failures. Now he had reached the end of his rope. He had lost everything, his money, his ministry, his marriage, his faith, everything, including God. With the Psalmist's cry on his lips he plunged into the ugly waters and began to swim out to sea, intending to keep going until the waves swallowed him, but suddenly in a thunderous flash he stopped and cried out, "Good God! What am I doing?" With despairing strength he swam back to the shore, sat down on a rock and broke into a convulsion of weeping. There came to his mind the image of his devout mother with the little catechism book in her hand, asking him, "Who is Jesus Christ?" Aloud he said, "Jesus Christ is my Saviour," and with those words a deep peace surged through his whole being. This man, the late D. R. Davies, found God where he least expected to find him—in deep despair. He writes, "In the final anguish, hovering between life and death, I found myself, as I was, and in my utter nakedness and worthlessness I found God."[1]

Is it possible that God purposely hides himself *so that we might be driven to an exercise of true faith?* What need for faith if God were always visible? The New Testament defines faith as "the assurance of things hoped for, the conviction of things not seen". Donald Hankey restated that definition when he wrote from a trench in Flanders in 1914, "Faith is betting your life there is a God." It does not take much of a gamble to believe that there is a God when the sun is shining and you can see signs of him on every hand, but when the sun goes behind the clouds and God goes with it, belief does become a gamble. It turns to faith; either that, or it dies. Faith is the last-ditch stand of religion. It is the stubborn persistence of belief in God when everything in our own lives and in the life of the world seems to contradict that belief. That is why we must think it possible that there are times, even troublous times, when God purposely hides himself so that we might be driven to an exercise of true faith.

In his autobiography Dr. F. W. Boreham, a great Australian preacher, writes proudly and gratefully of his parents. He tells that there was a time during his boyhood when he and his brothers noticed that their father looked anxious and worried and that their mother's eyes were often red and swollen. Suddenly the atmosphere changed, and it all had to do with a scrap of paper which had been cut from the corner of a penny sheet-almanac and fixed to the wall. Printed on it was a verse from the Bible: "Hitherto hath the Lord helped us." This tiny text made such a difference in the home that the boys finally mustered up

[1] D. R. Davies, *In Search of Myself* (Geoffrey Bles, London, 1961), pp. 189–90.

courage to ask their mother what it was all about. She told them:

> "Father and I have had a crushing trouble, and we feared a much heavier one. On Tuesday of last week I was feeling dreadfully worried. I had to drop my work, pick up the baby and walk up and down the kitchen feeling that I could endure it no longer. My burden was heavier than I could bear; it seemed to be killing me. In pacing up and down I paused for a second in front of the sheet-almanac on the wall. The only thing I saw was the text in the corner. I felt as if it had been put there specially for me. It was as if someone had spoken the words: *'Hitherto hath the Lord helped us.'* I was so overcome that I sat down and had a good cry; and then I began again with fresh heart and trust. When father came home I told him all about it, and he cut out the text with his penknife, had it framed and hung it where you now see it."

Writing fifty years afterwards Dr. Boreham says, "It was then that I made my discovery. Here was the secret! Here was the connection between religion and real life . . ."[1]

Here is the basis of what the Bible means by faith. Instead of pacing the floor and shouting to God, "Why hidest thou thyself in times of trouble?", faith means sitting down serenely, remembering that God has helped us in the past and trusting that he will see us through the problems troubling us now. Faith is not a way of whistling in the dark. It is a way of looking at the future with calm confidence that the God who has vindicated his holy name in the past is "King for ever and ever" and will keep all things in our lives and in the life of the world under his sovereign control. No man really comes close to God until he finds him by faith, and no man begins to exercise true faith until God seems to be hidden from his sight. That could be one very providential reason why God hides himself.

Is it possible that God purposely hides himself *so that we may rise to a higher level of spiritual perception?* There was a graduate student at Oxford who came away from his supervisor's office feeling dreadfully despondent. The supervisor told him that he had exhausted all the available English literature on his subject and that he would now have to read the untranslated

[1] F. W. Boreham, *My Pilgrimage.*

works of German scholars. "But sir," the student protested, "I don't know German." With Oxford casualness the supervisor replied, "Then it would seem that you will have to take time out to learn it. You have gone as far as you can go otherwise." Sometimes I think that God may say the same thing to one of us: "My child, you and I have gone as far as we can go on your present level of spiritual development. Therefore I am withdrawing myself from you for a time. When you have wrestled a bit and prayed and studied and deepened your understanding of Christian truth, then we shall come together again and move forward."

What does it mean? That we should go to Church more often or join a discussion group or read books on theology? If only it were that simple! Isaiah came closer to the reason for God's apparent absence when he warned the Jews, "Your iniquities have made a separation between you and your God, and your sins have hid his face from you . . .". It was the prophet's way of telling his people that they did not see God because they had destroyed their own competence to see God. He went on to tell them that pride, gluttony, deceit and dishonesty had blinded the eyes of their souls, so that they could not see God even if he stood directly in front of them. Jesus said that the pure in heart shall see God. He found God in all things—in the flowers of the field, children at play, labourers in a vineyard, women at their work, a shepherd seeking his sheep— and he promised that, though God may not always be accessible to the quick-witted or the clear-headed, he is never hidden from the eyes of the morally pure. "Blessed are the pure in heart: for they shall see God."

The pure in heart saw God in Jesus himself. It must have been difficult to discern the Almighty God in a helpless baby lying in a Bethlehem barn, but some humble shepherds, who were pure in heart, offered him their adoration. It must have been more difficult to recognize Creation's Lord in a Galilean carpenter, but peasants and fishermen and little children, who were pure in heart, fell at his feet in worship. It must have been most difficult to see the King of Heaven in a Man dying on a Cross, but there were those of pure heart even on Calvary who saw that he was about to inherit his Kingdom. This strange spiritual perception had very little to do with the way that people thought but it had everything to do with the way that people lived.

Not their minds but their characters opened their eyes to the presence of God in Jesus, and the purer their characters, the more vivid their vision of God.

Martin Luther has a favourite phrase in his writings. He refers to God as "the hidden God", the idea being that God always remains hidden unless and until he takes the initiative and makes himself known. The New Testament was written to show us that God has done exactly that in Jesus Christ. Once and for all God has broken the silence of heaven, stepped out from behind the clouds of mystery, entered our human scene and declared himself to be with us and among us forever. This is the truth that we celebrate at Christmas, the truth that our God is a "hidden God" no longer. After Christmas we need never again cry out with the Old Testament Psalmist, "Why standest thou afar off, O Lord? why hidest thou thyself in times of trouble?"

GOD SUFFICES

The *16th Psalm* is one of those Hebrew poems which is so candid in character that the poet's personality shines through every verse. Its mood of sheer delight climbs to such a crescendo of exuberant joy that you realize it could have been written only by a supremely happy man. You have the feeling that he must be the happiest man in the Bible.

> *"Preserve me, O God, for in thee I take refuge.*
> *I say to the Lord, 'Thou art my Lord;*
> *I have no good apart from thee'."*[1]

It recalls a light-hearted song from George Gershwin's *Porgy and Bess:* "I've got plenty of nothing . . . but I've got my Lord." This Hebrew poet had plenty of nothing—no money, no property, no status and no security—but he had God, and that made him happy. Like all the Psalmists of Israel he learned from his own experience an important truth about God, and in his case it was the truth that *God suffices.* If a man has God he can be happy, though he may not have much else. Without God, nothing else can make him happy. God alone gives him the ingredients of happiness, and the Psalm shows what those ingredients are.

> *"The Lord is my chosen portion and my cup;*
> *thou holdest my lot.*
> *The lines have fallen for me in pleasant places;*
> *Yea, I have a goodly heritage."*

What a sharp contrast to the prevailing mood of our day! An Englishman began a letter to the editor of *The Times* by saying, "I have recently returned after an absence of ten months to this lovely and beloved country to find, as it seems to me, a nation of grumblers." The writer catalogued some of the grumbles: "There is too much rain. There is not enough rain . . . The rates are too high. The roads are too full. The beaches

[1] This chapter follows the text of the Revised Standard Version.

are filthy . . . And the telephone service! And the trains! And the shop assistants! . . ." Trying to diagnose the mood of discontent the writer suggested that it might be the psychological aftermath of finding ourselves a second-class power or partly the result of being an "affluent society". He was very certain that "if we do not have the sense—if only the sense of humour—to snap out of it soon, a more dismal fate will overtake us." He closed with a bit of advice from the immortal wisdom of Bruce Bairnsfather, "If you knows of a better 'ole, go to it!"[1]

But that's just the trouble. Many people are, in fact, looking for a better 'ole. They are not satisfied with the present one. They believe that life has handed them a raw deal. They wish they had been born in some other century and some other country, of different parents and different social background, with greater gifts and better opportunities. They do not feel that the lines have fallen for them in pleasant places and that they have a goodly heritage. On the contrary, they feel cheated, badly-used and deprived, thoroughly dissatisfied and therefore utterly unhappy.

They may not believe it, but a change of scenery won't make them feel any better. There is no illusion more pathetic than the idea that, if we can just juggle a few things around and jockey ourselves into the perfect situation, we shall find the contented feeling which has hitherto eluded us. To begin with, there is no perfect situation. Then also, contentment is a state of mind; it flows from the inside out, not from the outside in. That is why men have found contentment in some very imperfect places. Paul found it in a prison cell where he wrote to his friends at Philippi, "I have learned, in whatever state I am, to be content." Describing the hardships and dangers of his life during the Nazi occupation, a leader of the Norwegian underground said in a kind of wonderment that one day it came to him that even in this hellish existence he was what men would call a happy man.

The Psalmist felt satisfied because he had God—"The Lord is my chosen portion and my cup . . ." A cynic may murmur something about "compensation" and religion being an "opiate", and he may declare that, if this pious poet had only possessed a few of the good things of life which are within man's power to provide for himself, he would not have needed God. The cynic, whatever doctrinaire axe he has to grind,

[1] June 17, 1965.

betrays a naïve ignorance of human nature. He supposes that the so-called "good things of life" can in fact meet man's deepest needs. He does not know that, when God created man, he left him unfinished within and gave him thirsts which God alone can quench and hungers which God alone can satisfy. Augustine saw more deeply into human nature when he confessed to God, "Thou hast made us for thyself, and our souls are restless until they find their rest in thee." The Psalmist found his rest in God. Therefore he was content and he asked nothing more of life. That was the effect of God in his experience.

> "I bless the Lord who gives me counsel;
> in the night also my heart instructs me."

A great deal of unhappiness arises out of sheer perplexity. It has been my experience as a pastor that most people who come to my vestry are seeking help in reaching their decisions and planning their future. One man cannot decide whether he ought to hang on to a secure job that he dislikes or take the venture of faith and emigrate to a new job abroad. A woman with a brute of a husband feels that she must leave him but is not sure if it is the right thing to do. These people are in mental anguish. They want somebody to make up their minds for them; and some counsellors, medical or legal or clerical, are willing to do it. For my part I believe that each man has to work out his own salvation and, though I may try to help him to see his predicament more clearly, I hesitate to play God in his life.

But God does not hesitate to play God. He played exactly that role in the Psalmist's experience. Presumably this man prayed in his perplexity, and from his prayer there came a sense of direction which made him absolutely certain that he was being Divinely guided. "I will bless the Lord who gives me counsel." One hears this grateful witness echoed all through the Bible; it begins with Abraham who heard God's voice calling him to Canaan; it continues to Paul who felt the Spirit of God directing him on his missionary journeys. It is a fact of universal human experience that, when a man lives close to God and honestly desires to do the will of God, he can count on God to counsel him.

A psychologist would be fascinated by the Psalmist's phrase, "in the night also my heart instructs me." Hebrew psychology saw the heart as the seat of man's moral nature, and the inference is that, even while we sleep, God counsels us by sensitizing our consciences to his will. This is not far-fetched when you remember that people have actually learned foreign languages and responded to suggestion made to them by means of recording devices wired to their beds while they were asleep. The idea does not help my insomnia but it offers a clue to the way that God can counsel us even in our sleep. The Bible does help our insomnia because it tells us not to lie awake worrying about our problems but to commit our perplexities to God, confident that, while the conscious mind rests, God will deal with us in our subconscious, giving us even as we sleep the wisdom, the guidance and the counsel that will help us to make the next day's decisions. That should be the effect of God in our experience.

"*I keep the Lord always before me;*
    because he is at my right hand, I shall not be moved."
Commentators dwell on the symbolism of the "right hand", reminding us that in the marriage ceremony the bridegroom stands at the right of his bride as a pledge of protection. A soldier's bodyguard stands at his right side, protecting him with his shield arm and leaving his sword arm free to deal with the enemy. The picture in the Psalm is that of a pilgrim walking behind the shield of God, while God has his sword unsheathed in his strong right arm to smite down the pilgrim's foes. To the Psalmist God has proved himself this kind of Defender, and the knowledge of it gives him a sense of stability.

It seems to me that every man has two ways of safeguarding his own happiness. As the first alternative let him make certain that he never runs into any kind of danger. Let him map out an itinerary for life's journey that will take him over no high mountains and through no deep valleys, over no rough roads and into no enemy territory. I have yet to meet a man who has been able to plan this ideal journey without finding his route going round in meaningless circles. People who travel to interesting places usually have to get there by tortuous paths, and all the way they have to be on constant guard against the assaults of their enemies. Only one thing can safeguard their happiness, and that is an inner sense of stability such as the

Psalmist possessed when he said of God, "because he is at my right hand, I shall not be moved."

Lawrence Zellers was one of a group of missionaries taken captive during the Korean War and interned for two years by the Communists. In a magazine article, written after his release and published in *The Christian Century*, he unfolded a ghastly chronicle of fear, depravity, suffering, disease, suicide and death. Yet he could say, "I look back on these years in captivity as one of the most rewarding periods, from a spiritual point of view, in my life." He told how noticeable was the difference between the prisoners who had spiritual fibre and those who lacked it. The latter gave up easily, lost all hope, sought refuge in suicide, especially in the winter of 1950 when death came simply by missing three or four meals. The Christian also faced this temptation and would have given in except, as Mr. Zellers said, "that he had a Power stronger than himself, even stronger than the influence of the Communism which held him captive, and this Power was reaching down to the depths of his soul supplying him with the will to carry on." Stability—that was the effect of God in the Christian's experience.

> "*Therefore my heart is glad, and my soul rejoices;*
> *my body also dwells secure.*
> *For thou dost not give me up to Sheol,*
> *or let thy godly one see the Pit.*"

The Psalm as a whole appeals to me in the *Revised Standard Version*, but at this point we cherish the older *King James Version* which reads, "For thou wilt not leave my soul in hell; neither wilt thou suffer thine Holy One to see corruption." Peter quoted this verse on the Day of Pentecost as a prophecy of God's mighty act in raising his Son from the dead. Paul caught its overtones when he articulated the eternal hope of all Christian believers: "For this corruptible must put on incorruption, and this mortal must put on immortality." Living in the light of Christ's resurrection, Paul had greater grounds for certainty than the Psalmist had, and that makes it all the more remarkable that a man who lived five hundred years before Christ should hold such a hope and in it find happiness.

There are people, many of them very intelligent, who would deny that hope of some future life is in any way essential to happiness in this life. Bertrand Russell writes quite cheerfully, "I believe that when I die I shall rot, and nothing of my ego will survive," but I think that a Broadway play, *The Best Man*, came closer to the longings of the human heart. The plot centres around a struggle for the United States Presidency. At one point in the dialogue an ageing ex-President asks one of the candidates, "Bill, do you believe in God?" The candidate replies stiffly that he was confirmed in the Episcopal Church. "That wasn't what I asked," says the older man. "I'm a Methodist and I'm still asking: do you believe there is a God and a Day of Judgment and a Hereafter?" Both politicians agree that they do not believe and that all this pious jargon, though useful for political campaigning, is just so much mythology. Then the ex-President confesses that he is dying of cancer and he says, "I tell you, son, I am scared to death . . . I don't fancy being just a pinch of dust." The young candidate tries to console him with his own brand of piety about the immortality of influence. To which the older man replies dryly, "I suggest you tell yourself that when you finally have to face a whole pile of nothin' up ahead."[1]

What reason have we to suppose that we shall not finally have to face a whole pile of nothin' up ahead? We have Christ, but the Psalmist did not have Christ. He had only hope, yet it was hope that amounted to more than wishful thinking because it was hope rooted and grounded in his experience of God. This is still the unshakeable basis of the soul's invincible surmise that God will not leave the soul in hell nor suffer it to see corruption. So far as we know, the soul, or the conscious personality, is still God's highest creation, still the crown and flower of the evolutionary process wrought through the agony of a million, million years; and if personality be lost in the mere decay of our organic system, then what seems like God's purpose for human life is nothing but a cosmic farce. Most of us would say with John Fiske, the Harvard scholar, "I believe in the immortality of the soul as a supreme act of faith in the reasonableness of God's work." The Psalmist had God in life; he hoped that he would have God after death. That hope was the result of God in his experience.

[1] Gore Vidal, *The Best Man*, reprinted in *Theatre Arts* by permission of Little, Brown and Co., New York.

"Thou dost show me the path of life;
in thy presence there is fullness of joy,
in thy right hand are pleasures for evermore."

We could strip away the rest of the Psalm, and this closing verse alone would mark down its author as the happiest man in the Bible. Any man, who can sing from his heart about "the path of life" and "fullness of joy" and "pleasures for evermore", is obviously a happy man whether he writes his song to be accompanied by shepherds' pipes or electric guitars. Any man who can praise God for this ecstatic mood of joy and jubilation is obviously a man who has found his happiness in God.

How many people today can take such a song on their lips and mean it? If they expressed their inmost feelings, would it not be in some mournful blues tune that told of how they have missed the path of life and failed to find fullness of joy and of how permanent pleasures have eluded them? They are unhappy, and at the root of their unhappiness lies a sense of unfulfilment. When Norman Cousins, the American journalist, visited Albert Schweitzer, he said that he came away with the impression of a man who had learned to use himself fully.[1] It occurred to Cousins that much of the ache and brooding unhappiness in life is the result of man's inability to use himself fully. Rarely do we realize our God-given potential, rarely do we release the yearnings and the powers of our personalities, rarely do we have a sense of fulfilling ourselves through total contact with total challenge. Therefore we are not happy.

Is it really true that God makes a difference and that, if we believe in God and obey him, he will give us a sense of being usefully and joyfully alive? Not if we confuse God with religion and make him a mere appendage to our lives like bird-watching and going to the theatre. We have to think of God not only as a Person to be worshipped but as an environment to be lived in. Notwithstanding the fact that happiness flows from the inside out, there is no need to argue that environment can make a difference to our happiness. A man moves from one locality to another and, though he may be doing the same work and be married to the same wife, the new surroundings so suit his temperament and release his potential that all his

---

[1] Norman Cousins, *Dr. Schweitzer of Lambarene* (Harper and Brothers, Publishers, New York, 1960).

relationships are suffused with new meaning and joy. That should be the effect of God in man's experience. Outwardly things may remain unchanged, but when all of life—its loves and labours and duties—is set in the light of God and made an act of obedience to God, then God himself gives to life a sense of permanent and joyous fulfilment.

Some years ago a man said to me, "I have never been happier in my life!" That was a strange thing to say under the circumstances, because he had just resigned a highly-paid job to enter a new line of work that would never give him more than a quarter of his former salary. The change would make most people quite miserable. Yet he really meant it when he said, "I have never been happier in my life!" The reason for his new-found happiness was that he had discovered God and had offered his life in obedience to the purpose of God. He really believed that for the first time in his life he was doing what God wanted him to do. And he was happy. That made him a kindred spirit with the writer of the 16th Psalm who learned from his own experience that, when a man has God, he does not need much else, because God alone can give him contentment, guidance, stability, hope and fulfilment—the ingredients of happiness.

GOD CARES

In one of my congregations there was a saintly woman, well past her ninetieth year, who kept coaxing me to preach a sermon on the *23rd Psalm*. I used to think, Why should it be necessary? A child can understand this simple Psalm which, next to the Lord's Prayer, makes up the most beloved and most quoted half-dozen verses in all Scripture. To explain it to a congregation of mature Christians would be like teaching the multiplication tables to a class of university students. Even those "fugitive fringe" Christians, who are so ignorant of the Bible that they think that Dan and Beersheba were brother and sister, can probably recite "*The Lord is my shepherd*" and, in doing so, find it a source of inspiration and comfort. They may not understand much else in the Bible, but surely the meaning of this familiar Psalm is obvious to them.

But is it so obvious? The dear old lady may have known better. Perhaps she realized that, precious as the 23rd Psalm is to a great many people, yet they have never grasped its truth as a relevant Word of God. One reason for this could be that they have never managed to get beyond the archaic imagery of the shepherd and his sheep. A few years ago the *Readers Digest*[1] published a helpful interpretation of this Psalm as given by a Basque shepherd. He went through it verse by verse and showed how the shepherd still cares for his sheep exactly as he did on the Judean hills thirty centuries ago. It was a beautiful and fascinating piece. It explained the imagery but said almost nothing about the truth behind the imagery, and, though we were charmed by it, we ended up knowing more about sheep than about God.

The 23rd Psalm is a sublime poem about God. It is one man's testimony but it testifies to the reality of God in every man's experience. The author, because he is a shepherd, thinks of how he cares for his sheep, and the conviction floods his mind that *God cares* for his people in exactly the same way. Just as

[1] June 1950.

the shepherd accepts responsibility for each animal in his charge, so God cares for every person as though he cared for that person alone. Just as the shepherd cares actively for his sheep, so God does not watch over us passively but involves himself in our lives to lead and comfort and rescue and restore. Just as the shepherd is concerned for the total welfare of his flock, so God is concerned for all our physical, mental, emotional, moral and spiritual needs. The whole range of man's experience comes under God's watchful and loving care—*this* is the truth of the 23rd Psalm.

Would you call it an obvious truth? Obvious it may be, but many people have never seen it or else have lost sight of it. A recent public opinion poll in Britain showed that, of some 2,200 people interviewed, four out of every five said that they believe in a God of some kind. One in five goes to church, and most churchgoers say that they believe in a personal God.[1] They believe with their minds; whether they believe with their lives is another matter. They may assent to God's existence and still be practical atheists. They may believe that God is personal but not a Person with whom they have to do. They may stoutly affirm that they are people of deep religious faith while everything about their lives seems to deny a deep religious faith.

Their *excessive anxiety* denies it. Anxiety may be too strong and broad a term if we understand it in its medical sense as an emotional illness which shows itself in various forms of hysteria. A more accurate word is "worry", but we call it "anxiety" because Jesus called it such when he said to the disciples, "Therefore do not be anxious, saying, 'What shall we eat?' or 'What shall we drink?' or 'What shall we wear?'" Jesus did not say "Stop worrying about the necessities of life" but he did imply that the man who worries himself sick over them is really a practical atheist. That man may believe in God but he does not believe in a personal God who cares for his creatures and provides for their needs. Reminding his disciples that even the birds of the air and the flowers of the field live by the generosity of their Creator, Jesus said, "Are you not of more value than they . . . O men of little faith?"

The author of the 23rd Psalm was a man of great faith. In

[1] Television and Religion (published by the University of London Press Ltd., Copyright A.B.C. Television Ltd., 1964).

fact, he was really an incredible person. "*My cup runneth over*," he said—and that in a day before welfare state programmes, life insurance, pension schemes, penicillin, blood plasma and bottled oxygen. We could understand his sense of security if he had been a wealthy man, but he was not a wealthy man, at least in terms of the material affluence which in his day, as in ours, constituted wealth. He was probably a farmer trying to eke a living out of badly-irrigated land that yielded an uncertain harvest, a shepherd depending for his livelihood on flocks that were constantly exposed to the perils of disease and storms and wild beasts. Yet he did not worry to a point of anxiety because he believed that in a world governed by a personal, caring God his material needs would be met. "*The Lord is my shepherd; I shall not want*"—such was the effect of God in this man's experience.

That many people today do not believe in a personal, caring God is evident from their *sense of inadequacy* to the stresses and strains of life. A newspaper article, headlined "Metal Fatigue", told the tragic story of an aircraft which crashed with forty-one Service-men on board because of a failure in the elevator support system due to metal fatigue. At first glance I thought the headline said "Mental Fatigue", because it is one of the tragic features of the hectic pace of life in our jet-propelled age that more and more people are crashing under the strain. Our great problem today is that of restoring our energies, renewing the strength of our bodies and souls, finding a sense of adequacy to the stresses and strains of life.

With some people the problem is so pressing that they turn to irrational solutions. They drink to excess, they take tranquillizer pills with or without a doctor's prescription, they find release in drugs and sometimes they get "hooked". In his remarkable book, *Come Out the Wilderness*, Bruce Kenrick quotes this terrible parody on the 23rd Psalm written by a young drug addict in New York's East Harlem:

"Heroin is my shepherd
I shall not want
It maketh me to lie down in gutters
It leadeth me beside still madness
It destroyeth my soul

C

It leadeth me in the paths of Hell for its name's sake
Yea, though I walk through the Valley of the Shadow of
  Death
I will fear no evil
For heroin art with me
My syringe and spike shall comfort me
Thou puttest me to shame in the presence of mine enemies
Thou anointest my head with madness
My cup runneth over with sorrow
Surely hate and evil shall follow me all the days of my life
And I will dwell in the house of misery and disgrace for ever."[1]

The Psalmist, though he lived in a simpler age than ours, faced the problem of stress and found his answer in God. He gives us a tender picture of One who looks at the needs of all his children and, seeing them tense and tired, leads them to the place of rest and refreshment. "*He maketh me to lie down in green pastures: he leadeth me beside the still waters. He restoreth my soul.*"

That is how many people have experienced God in their lives. You meet them and marvel at their prodigious energy, their tireless labour, their prolific output of work, and you marvel even more that they move with such poise, always relaxed, never dissipating their strength, always human beings and never machines. It is revealing how many of the world's busiest men have stood up under stress only because they found rest and refreshment in God. Such a man was Dr. Paul Carlson, medical missionary, who was massacred by rebels in the African Congo. He had been the only doctor serving a hundred thousand people, treating hundreds of patients a week and performing at least one major operation a day. How did he stand the strain without giving way to mental fatigue? His wife said that she thought it was the result of his having kept close to God through prayer and meditation and study of the Bible. On the day before his execution Dr. Carlson wrote a single word in his pocket New Testament, the word "Peace". That was the effect of God in his experience.

People betray their practical atheism in *a sense of moral confusion*. In the journal *Christianity and Crisis*, Robert E. Fitch describes what he calls "the obsolescence of ethics":

[1] Collins Fontana Books, London, 1965, p. 163.

"We live today in an age when ethics is becoming obsolete. It is superseded by science, deleted by psychology, dismissed as emotive by philosophy; it is drowned in compassion, evaporates into aesthetics and retreats before relativism."

It may be true that we are witnessing a breakdown of moral standards, but it is also true that behind a great deal of the immorality of our day there is not so much downright badness as sincere confusion about what is good. Most of us want to do the right thing in life and to maintain what someone has called "the moral grandeur of independent integrity", but our values are distorted by such complicating factors as the pathological reaction to Puritanism and the mingling of different cultures in our great cities. We need guidance in life, signposts that point in the right direction and, most of all, an inner impulse that will help us to walk in the right direction.

In the Psalmist's life God met that need. It was not simply that this Hebrew poet had God's moral laws to guide him but that he found the living God to be the most potent factor in his struggle to obey those laws: "*He leadeth me in the paths of righteousness for his name's sake.*" At this point the 23rd Psalm pictures God not as a shepherd but as a Father. A wise and loving human father, though he does not force his son in the direction of truth and honour and goodness, will encourage him in that direction, not for the boy's sake only but for his own sake. The father's good name stands or falls by his son's behaviour, and for the sake of his own reputation he leads his son in the paths of righteousness.

It is a daring picture but one that is entirely consistent with God as men have experienced him. In their moral struggles they have prayed, as Jesus taught us to pray, "Lead us not into temptation, but deliver us from evil," and in ways they could never have imagined the path of righteousness has been made plain and the impulse to walk in it has been unmistakable. One evening a top-level delegation waited upon Abraham Lincoln at the White House and warned him that, unless he abandoned his anti-slavery campaign, he would lose the support of his entire cabinet. The President listened patiently and promised to give his answer next morning. History knows what that answer was: "No nation can endure half-slave and half-free."

Lincoln spent the night on his knees, and God led him in the paths of righteousness for his name's sake.

Faith in a living, personal God might save many people from their *uncontrollable panic* in the face of great danger. "*Yea, though I walk through the valley of the shadow of death, I will fear no evil: for thou art with me; thy rod and thy staff they comfort me.*" What a complete picture of life the Psalmist paints. He takes in everything—the hills and the valleys, the lights and the shadows, the sun-swept pastures and the dark defile. In picturesque language he proclaims his faith that God is the Lord of all life and that not a single one of our human experiences fails to come within his providence. In all of them God meets us and plays a part.

Look at the verse, "*Thou preparest a table before me in the presence of mine enemies: thou anointest my head with oil . . .*" I have often thought that it must have been very real during the war when Christian people in Britain came to church after a bombing raid and sat down to a sacramental meal at the Lord's Table. God did not protect them against their enemies but he did sustain and comfort them in the presence of their enemies. That is the effect of God in our experience—to protect us not against danger but against fear, not against hurt but against cynicism, not against failure but against the pessimism that failure brings, not against illness and disease but against the spirit of murmuring and complaining, not against bereavement and sorrow but against hopelessness and despair.

From the 23rd Psalm Bishop Hans Lilje, one of the heroes of the German Resistance Movement, took the title of his inspiring book, *The Valley of the Shadow*[1] where he describes his experiences in a Nazi concentration camp. Repeatedly he tells that you could distinguish between the prisoners who possessed a conviction of God and those who lacked it. The first group were simply not afraid any more; they had conquered their fears, even the fear of death. Lilje himself tells that, though he expected to face the firing squad any day, yet because he had thought about death in the light of his Christian faith, even the bars on his window and the chains on his wrists seemed no longer to have much meaning. He writes:

[1] Translated by Olive Wyon (The Muhlenberg Press, Philadelphia, 1950).

"In those days it was granted to me to tread the shores of that land which lies on the outermost fringe of time, upon which already something of the radiance of the other world is shining. I did not know that an existence which is still earthly and human could be so open to the world of God. It was a stillness full of blessing, a solitude over which God brooded, an imprisonment blessed by God Himself."

The absence of faith in a personal, caring God shows itself in the *sense of futility* with which some people confront life. In a theatre magazine I read a rather discerning review of a play. The critic began by commending the leading actors and by praising the production in some of its scenes. Then he examined the piece itself, complimenting the author for occasional flashes of genius but ending with the devastating verdict that, while there were unmistakable meanings *in* it, the play as a whole had no significant meaning *to* it. Sometimes people say the same thing about life: it has meaning but no ultimate meaning. Its scenes and episodes are significant, but life as a whole, the complete drama, the story from beginning to end—that adds up to nothing.

The reason for this sense of futility is not difficult to find. There was a time when Spain stamped on her coins the Pillars of Hercules and underneath them the inscription, *Ne Plus Ultra*, meaning "No More Beyond". That is what many people say when they come to the end of life—"No more beyond; nothing on the other side of the blank wall of death"; and if the end of life is nothing, then life itself, the preface to that end, is nothing. But the picture can change and sometimes does change. Columbus discovered a new world far beyond the Pillars of Hercules, so the Spanish government deleted the *ne* and left the *plus ultra*, meaning "More beyond". One thing can save life from futility—hope that there is more beyond, hope that the lives, the loves and the labours begun in time do not end in time but find their fulfilment in eternity.

We have that hope if we believe in God; it is the effect of God in man's experience. The writer of the 23rd Psalm lived a long time before the Pioneer of our Faith came back to tell us about a new world far beyond the bounds of vision but, like many of the Psalmists, he had intimations of the immortality that God brought to light in Christ. How, indeed, could he resist the conviction? When he remembered how God had brought him into the world and watched over him and provided for his needs and met him at every turn of the way and never failed him, it seemed unthinkable that this loving, caring God should desert him at death. The God who had played a part in his every experience would surely not fail to play a part in the greatest experience of all. Looking at death a different way, the Psalmist began looking at life in a different way until its meaning and joy flooded his soul and he cried out in faith, "*Surely goodness and mercy shall follow me all the days of my life: and I will dwell in the house of the Lord for ever.*"

So he was right, eternally right, this Hebrew poet who portrayed God as the Divine Shepherd watching over his sheep, caring personally and actively with a care that encompasses all our lives and reaches even beyond death. How do we know? We know because of One who called himself the Good Shepherd and had a right to do so because he was to men all that the Psalmist believed God to be. Jesus Christ is the Good Shepherd, and that tells us all that we need to know about God, because Jesus Christ *is* God in man's experience.

GOD HEARTENS

A picture in a popular magazine showed hundreds of people on a busy street corner going about their daily affairs. You could see a mother with two children, her arms filled with parcels, and worry written on her face. You could see a business man rushing into a bank, evidently annoyed at missing the first section of a revolving door. You could see a youth leaning against a building, apparently with no place to go, whose eyes betrayed a sense of boredom and discontent. The caption read, "Of what are these people afraid?"

It was a fair question, because most people, even those with strong and aggressive personalities, harbour some secret fears. They may be afraid of the dark or of dizzy heights or of big crowds or of small spaces. Psychology has coined a whole new jargon to describe our fears, endless variations on the Greek word *phobia*. Consult the phobias listed in a modern dictionary. They total more than seventy-five, ranging all the way from ereuthophobia, the fear of blushing, to phobophobia, the fear of fear itself—and that is not imaginary, because, as President Roosevelt declared during the Second World War, "The only thing we have to fear is fear".

Addressing the National Association of Mental Health in London, a distinguished psychologist, Professor G. M. Carstairs of Edinburgh University, said that fear is the great threat to mental health in our generation. He catalogued some genuine fears that unnerve us and play havoc with our peace of mind. First and most obvious, there is the fear of the bomb. Said Professor Carstairs, "We live in a world where the lunatic dialogue of 'if you blow me up, I will blow you up' has become a serious reality. Our children are living in a folklore of bombs." Then there is the fear of unemployment which becomes increasingly acute as machines do the work of men, and the fear of failure which haunts a child from the day when he writes his first examinations in school. Many people in middle-age fear a break-down in health, and most people, as they grow older, have some fear of death. Thus the litany of fear might be extended indefinitely, the cry, "Good Lord, Deliver us!" gathering intensity with each item.

Fear is not a sign of cowardice; it does not denote an absence of courage. When a demolition officer had removed the fuse from a land mine and rendered it harmless, a friend gasped in admiration, "How can you do that kind of thing without being afraid?" The officer wiped the perspiration from his face and said, "Every time I am called to one of these jobs I am afraid." Of course he was afraid. His fear kept him alert to the danger. Fear is an essential emotion that plays a preventive and constructive role in life. It is part of the process of growing up. Unless a child develops a few healthy fears like the fear of speeding cars, boiling kettles, deep water and bottles labelled "poison", he may not have a chance to grow up. Nor is fear the same thing as anxiety. Anxiety is an abnormal state of mind which exists without a specific cause and may turn a man into a neurotic. The anxious man has a supply of anxiety stored up inside him; it may focus for a time on some acceptable object but, even if the object were removed, the anxiety would still be there. Fear, on the other hand, does have specific causes which can be faced, analysed, attacked, eliminated or endured. A man can deal with his fears.

The *27th Psalm* is the personal testimony of a man who learned to deal with his fears. Despite the strange alternation of moods, which support the theory that it may be a composite poem by more than one author, the Psalm as a whole does have a unifying theme in the relation of God to man's fear. Whoever he was, the Psalmist knew the meaning of fear. He had suffered all the symptoms—dry mouth, trembling hands, weak knees and fainting heart. These symptoms had not been brought on by any spectre of the imagination but by terrifying circumstances which were as real as an air raid, an earthquake, an armed robbery or a cancer operation. When his nerve failed him, the Psalmist did what many people do—he turned to God and, in so doing, made a tremendous discovery. He discovered that, though God does not always remove the causes of fear, he does give us the inward resources to deal with them. God puts courage into a man, strengthens his heart, stiffens his backbone and gives him a sense of spiritual guts. The God with whom we have to do is *a God who heartens*. Such was the effect of a living religion in the experience of the writer of the 27th Psalm.

The Psalmist's testimony begins where religion must always begin—with a declaration of personal faith:

"The Lord is my light and my salvation: whom shall I fear? the Lord is the strength of my life; of whom shall I be afraid?"

When a sudden storm threatened to swamp their fishing boat and send them to a watery grave in the Sea of Galilee, the disciples of Jesus were afraid, as we should be afraid under the same circumstances, so they wakened Jesus who was sleeping peacefully in the stern and cried out, "Teacher, do you not care if we perish?" Raising his arm, Jesus rebuked the wind and the waves, calling out, "Peace! Be still!" and, as the storm subsided, he turned to rebuke his fear-stricken disciples, saying, "Why are you afraid? Have you no faith?" Not that faith is supposed to be an antidote to fear. Jesus meant that, with him and therefore with God in their situation, the disciples should have been able to bring their fears under control. So it was with the Psalmist who now tells us the extent of his faith:

"Though an host should encamp against me, my heart shall not fear: though war should rise against me, in this will I be confident".

In reading the Psalm we must place our emphasis on the personal pronoun—"The Lord is *my* light and *my* salvation . . . the strength of *my* life . . ." The Psalmist is not preaching a sermon, not outlining a set of general propositions about religion. He is not trying to prove anything or speak for anyone except himself; and in this he provides a refreshing contrast to some agnostics who insist on generalizing their own doubts, like a blind man who says that there is no moon because he can't see the moon. Psalm 27 is a personal testimony, nothing more, nothing less. The author shares with us his own conviction about God and tells us how his religion has helped him to deal with his fears.

Religion *must* be a personal testimony, it must be an experience that happens to *us*, like falling in love or being cured of an illness, before we can relate it to our concerns and worries and fears. I always like to meet someone who wants to read books and listen to lectures and join in discussions and generally be informed about religion. However, I tell that person that, if he expects religion to be anything more than a subject of academic inquiry, if he wants it to make a real difference in his life and be a means of solving his problems, he will have to make the transition from second-hand knowledge to first-hand experience. He will have to stop talking about his religion and begin practising it.

John R. Mott, a great Christian layman who was the first Honorary President of the World Council of Churches, said that in his early years at university he began to have some serious doubts about the effectiveness of prayer. He didn't see how prayer could work, how it could change people or events outside the person who prays. To deal with his doubts Dr. Mott decided to read some books on prayer. He read forty-three in all and, though he found them enlightening, they did not resolve his doubts. At last he decided to try a different approach. He stopped reading and gave up his wearisome discussions on prayer and actually began to pray. He prayed regularly and fervently and discovered for himself the truth of Scripture that "the prayer of a righteous man has great power in its effects". Dr. Mott made the transition from a second-hand knowledge of religion to a first-hand experience of religion; and that is what *we* must do if we want our religion to make a real difference in our lives and be an effectual means of dealing with our fears.

The writer of the 27th Psalm goes on to describe his religious life. At one time the description might have seemed common-place but it suddenly becomes important in these days of secularization when men are debating what it means to be religious. Even some theologians no longer believe in a living God who exists outside the world which he has created and who works personally in human life and history. They tell us that God is not a Person who loves; God *is* love, the sum total of all the love in human life and history, and that we deal with this God not through the formal practice of religion but through loving involvement in the lives and affairs of men. Thus a man may be religious though he never goes to Church and though he never kneels down to pray. In this *avant-garde* view the Old Testament Psalmist is out of date; but out of date or not, he still has something to teach us, because his belief in a living, personal God and his conscious effort to live close to this living, personal God did for him what our modern semi-humanism singularly fails to do for a great many people—it worked, it put new heart into him and helped him to deal with his fears.

In the practice of his religion, which is no longer common-place, the Psalmist went to Church; he went regularly, humbly, reverently and faithfully:

"One thing have I desired of the Lord, that will I seek after; that I may dwell in the house of the Lord all the days of my life, to behold the beauty of the Lord, and to inquire in his temple."

Not only so, but he enjoyed going to the house of God:

"therefore will I offer in his tabernacle sacrifices of joy; I will sing, yea, I will sing praises unto the Lord."

Worshipping God was not a boring duty for the Psalmist. It strengthened him, comforted him and gave him a sense of stability:

"For in the time of trouble he shall hide me in his pavilion: in the secret of his tabernacle shall he hide me; he shall set me upon a rock."

There are still some old-fashioned folk like the Hebrew Psalmist who enjoy going to church, not because they want to escape from involvement in the world but because the experience of worship makes them equal to involvement in the world. A few years ago I conducted a brief pulpit ministry at St. Stephen's Church, Sydney, Australia. Every Wednesday noon a thousand people from the surrounding offices give up a part of their precious lunch-hour to attend the brief mid-week service. They come to the house of God out of a sense of human need. One Wednesday, after the service, a kind lady took me to a wool auction which seemed not unlike a congregation facing a preacher in a pulpit. (It occurred to me that, if the "religionless Christianity" trend continues and I become redundant as a minister, I can always get a job as an auctioneer.) When I tried to thank the lady, she spoke affectionately of her debt to St. Stephen's Church. She said, "I can't tell you what the Wednesday service means to me. After I come away I live on the memory of it, then I begin looking forward to next week's service. It does me good just to be a part of that great worshipping congregation. It gives me stability and hope and joy. It makes the rest of life worth while".

In the practice of religion the Psalmist said his prayers. The Psalm itself is the best possible proof of this because it contains a prayer of sublime and fervent devotion:

> "*Hear, O Lord, when I cry with my voice: Have mercy also upon me, and answer me.*"

We do well to study this prayer for two reasons. First, because we who have difficulty in praying can learn from it something about the anatomy of prayer, the effectual means of approach to God. It begins with a response to God's gracious invitation:

> "*When thou saidst, Seek ye my face; my heart said unto thee, Thy face, Lord, will I seek.*"

It is a prayer of dependent faith:

> "*Hide not thy face far from me; put not thy servant away in anger: thou hast been my help; leave me not, neither forsake me, O God of my salvation.*"

The Psalmist declares to God the extent of his faith:

> "*When my father and my mother forsake me, then the Lord will take me up.*"

It is a prayer of humble submission to God's will:

> "*Teach me thy way, O Lord, and lead me in a plain path, because of mine enemies.*"

And it is an honest confession of need and an earnest cry for help:

> "*Deliver me not over unto the will of mine enemies: for false witnesses are risen up against me, and such as breathe out cruelty.*"

Still more important, the Psalmist's prayer teaches us something about the spirit in which we ought to approach God. Studdert Kennedy, a great chaplain in the First World War, used to tell of listening to two frightened soldiers during a heavy bombardment on their trench. In occasional pauses between the immense crashings and howlings he heard a sergeant cursing vividly and he heard a man next to him who was despairing and shivering and praying aloud for safety. He said that he found the praying the more disgusting of the two, a disgust compounded by the realization that a great deal of the prayer, in peace as in war, was in fact of that order, if not of that urgency. Studdert Kennedy asked himself, "What, then, was prayer that was not contemptible or selfish or useless?" and he concluded that true prayer is that which asks not for permission to survive but for courage to endure. Such was the prayer of Jesus in Gethsemane.[1] Such was the prayer of the Psalmist, a prayer for courage to endure and, as such, it worked; it made a difference in his life; it strengthened him, put new heart into him and helped him to control his fears.

We return to the Psalmist's personal testimony, in which he tells us the precise difference that religion made in his life:

"*When the wicked, even mine enemies and my foes, came upon me to eat up my flesh, they stumbled and fell.*"

This may have been literally true. If the 27th Psalm is, as the title indicates, "A Psalm of David", we have only to read of his military campaigns in the Old Testament books of *Samuel* and *Chronicles* in order to test the truth of David's testimony. No sooner had he been crowned king of Israel and been acknowledged by other kings, than the lords of the Philistines, recognizing him as a threat, decided that they had better eliminate him, Twice they assembled their armies in the Valley of Rephaim, a mighty host over against the tiny army of Israel. Each time David prayed to God for guidance and each time by Divinely-inspired strategy he won a victory. He could say with literal truth that, when his enemies and his foes came upon him to eat up his flesh, they stumbled and fell.

This is true in a larger sense. Every man has enemies and foes, some of them wicked indeed, who come upon him to eat up his flesh, and their presence unnerves him and strikes fear into his heart. There are the ills that flesh is heir to, the dizzy spells or the pain in the chest that could denote advancing age or

[1] Told by William Purcell in *Woodbine Willie* (Hodder and Stoughton, London, 1962), p. 107.

could mean something more serious. What man has not trembled in a doctor's office as he awaited the results of an x-ray? There are the evil influences that assemble like an army around the fortress of a man's integrity from the time of his youth, the subtle temptations and lurid fantasies which may become a reality too strong to resist. There are the sudden misfortunes that never seem to come singly but in droves, threatening to smash our cherished security and to plunge us and our loved ones into irretrievable disaster. Yet it is one of the strange experiences of life lived close to God that many of the things, which we most feared, did not happen to us. Many times we have been like the citizens of ancient Jerusalem, besieged by the army of Assyria, cowering in terror as we waited for the blow to fall. Suddenly everything became quiet, and when we dared to look over the walls of the city we saw that the besieging army had disappeared. When our enemies and our foes came upon us to eat up our flesh, they stumbled and fell; and the memory of this past deliverance puts new heart into us now and helps us to deal with our present fears.

The Psalmist gives a more powerful testimony when he says,

"I had fainted, unless I had believed to see the goodness of the Lord in the land of the living."

"I had fainted"—that is the final symptom of fear: a complete collapse of spirit when terror so paralyzes the senses that a man's knees buckle beneath him and he capitulates into unconsciousness. He becomes so scared that he passes out. It happens to the toughest of men and it would have happened to the Psalmist but for the inward resources that reinforced his nerve and kept him on his feet. Evil raged like a storm all around him. The malignance of his enemies and the treachery of his friends beat upon his sensitive spirit like a hurricane, and he would have collapsed but for one thing—his belief in the goodness of God. That faith steadied him and brought him through the crisis.

It was late in the evening. At the end of a long, busy day I felt almost too tired to make my last pastoral visit. An elderly lady answered the door. I had not realized that she was one of the shut-ins of my new congregation or I would have called at an earlier hour. I decided that it would be a taxing visit and I wondered if I should have the energy to be of any help as a pastor. I need not have worried. The old lady put me at my ease. She seemed serene and contented. She smiled beautifully and spoke in a soft, soothing voice. I began to feel less tense and tired as I knew myself to be in the presence of a calm and radiant faith. She told me that she was not afraid to live by herself in the house, not afraid of illness, not afraid of dying. "I shall never be afraid of anything any more," she said and she told me the reason. For years she had nursed her invalid husband, always fearful to leave him lest he should die while she was not at his bedside. Once, when she retired to her own room completely exhausted, she lay there feeling the weight of her fear and praying about it when she seemed to hear a voice saying clearly and distinctly, "Do not be afraid." She believed that it was the voice of God, and though it probably spoke, as the voice of God *does* speak, through her imagination, it steadied her and brought her through her great crisis; and the memory of it helped her to deal with her present fears.

I got the impression that this elderly shut-in knew what she was talking about. I get the same impression about the writer of the 27th Psalm. He finds all of us in that magazine picture—afraid of something that might happen to us and perhaps unnerved by our fears. He knows that what we need most in life is an injection of courage, something that will steady our nerves, put new heart into us and keep us on our feet. So he ends his Psalm with a great admonition which we can take to heart because he is not arguing with us, not preaching at us but simply commending us to the God of his experience:

"*Wait on the Lord: be of good courage, and he shall strengthen thine heart: wait, I say, on the Lord.*"

GOD SPEAKS

H. G. Wells wrote a satirical short story about an Archbishop who ran into difficulty and decided to pray about it. He had always said his prayers with the utmost regularity. Prayer he regarded as a purifying, beneficial process, no more to be neglected than brushing his teeth. Yet he had never really asked God for anything. He had not made a particular and personal appeal to God on his own behalf for many years. In this tangle, however, he needed help desperately so, entering his private chapel, he sank to his knees and folded his hands. "O God," he began, and paused. He paused, and a sense of awful imminence gripped him, He heard a voice, not a harsh voice but a clear, strong voice, neither friendly nor hostile. "Yes," said the voice, "What is it?" They found His Grace next morning. He had slipped off the chancel steps and lay sprawling on the crimson carpet. Plainly, his death had been instantaneous. Many people would die of fright if ever they heard a voice in the secret place of prayer saying to them, "Yes, what is it?" The truth is that we do not expect that kind of response from God. We speak to God, we address him in public worship and private prayer, we call him by name and pour out our petitions, but not with any real sense of a Hearer listening to us at the other end of a telephone. Even if God does listen, we give him no chance to reply because, having finished our side of the conversation, we put the telephone down and walk away. We speak to God but we have never heard God speak to us.

Yet God does speak to us; He is speaking to us all the time. That is one of the great truths about God in man's experience. The Bible was written by men who heard God speak. "*The voice of the Lord is powerful*" declared the writer of the *29th Psalm*— a more meaningful declaration if he also wrote the 28th Psalm which begins with an impassioned protest against God's silence: "Unto thee will I cry, O Lord my rock; be not silent to me; lest, if thou be silent to me, I become like them that go down into the pit." Plainly, powerfully, God must have answered the Hebrew poet. Seven times in his brief Psalm he uses the phrase, "*the voice of the Lord.*" The Bible tells us of *a God who speaks*. More than that, it tells us how God speaks and where we can hear the voice of the Lord.

We can hear the voice of the Lord *speaking through nature.* The Psalmist does not simply declare this truth; he sings it in a majestic anthem of praise:

"*Give unto the Lord, O ye mighty, give unto the Lord glory and strength.*

Give unto the Lord the glory due unto his name; worship the Lord in the beauty of holiness.

The voice of the Lord is upon the waters: the God of glory thundereth: the Lord is upon many waters.

The voice of the Lord is powerful; the voice of the Lord is full of majesty.

The voice of the Lord breaketh the cedars; yea, the Lord breaketh the cedars of Lebanon.

He maketh them also to skip like a calf; Lebanon and Sirion like a young unicorn.

The voice of the Lord divideth the flames of fire.

The voice of the Lord shaketh the wilderness; the Lord shaketh the wilderness of Kadesh.

The voice of the Lord maketh the hinds to calve, and discovereth the forests: and in his temple doth every one speak of his glory.

The Lord sitteth upon the flood; yea, the Lord sitteth King for ever.

The Lord will give strength unto his people; the Lord will bless his people with peace."

The voice of God in nature is a theme that finds many an echo in the Psalter, especially the favourite and familiar 19th Psalm: "The heavens declare the glory of God; and the firmament showeth his handiwork. Day unto day uttereth speech, and night unto night sheweth knowledge. There is no speech nor language, where their voice is not heard." That last is literally true—"no speech nor language, where their voice is not heard." The same sun and the same moon shine on the Pope of Rome and the jungle witch doctor, and to each the sun and moon declare the glory of God. Above the confusion

D

of conflicting cultures and civilizations nature speaks to man its universal language and it speaks to him of God.

The Bible tells us that God himself actually speaks through nature. To the wretched Job, who blasphemously challenged God to a dialogue, God spoke through a whirlwind, sledging the sufferer with a barrage of questions about nature that stunned him into silence. What probably happened is that Job, sitting in solitary misery and brooding on the vastness and variety of nature, heard for the first time the voice of nature's Lord. We, too, if we listened to the natural world about us, might hear its overtones speaking to the needs of our human situation. Sunset and dawn, winter and summer might tell us that we live in an orderly, dependable world and that behind it is a Creative Spirit ever intelligent and supremely loving. The receding waves on the seashore might tell us, as they told Job, that the God who sets boundaries for the ocean tides also sets boundaries for the destructive elements that beat on the shore of man's soul. Looking at the mountain goat, we receive assurance that God who cares for the least of his creatures will also care for the noblest of his creatures; and from the wild flower in the desert we learn that God who lavishes love on the waste and desolate ground will not forget men and women in their waste and desolate hearts. The view of an expanding universe strengthens our faith as it reminds us that the God who controls the world in space can be trusted to control the world in history. Through nature the voice of God speaks, and that voice is very powerful.

The Bible tells us that we can hear the voice of the Lord *speaking through history*. At school I found history a dull subject, perhaps because I had dull teachers or more probably because I had a dull mind. I saw history as no more than a chronicle of events and dates to be memorized, then regurgitated on an examination paper. That is not how the writers of the Old Testament saw history. To them history was a fascinating drama, alive with meaning for their own day. Unceasingly they pointed their people to the past, recalling for them the events of the past through which they believed that God spoke to the present.

Sometimes the past speaks with a warning voice. The Book of *Judges*, made up of legends, folk tales and historical narrative, was written six centuries after the events which it relates.

To warn his people of the consequences of their defection from God the editor puts their history in a nutshell. He shows them how each generation passes through the same stages: first, the people worship God and obey him; second, they forsake the Lord and provoke him to anger; third, the Lord delivers them into the hands of their enemies; fourth, the people are distressed and cry to the Lord for help; fifth, the Lord has pity and saves his people. Thirteen times in this single period of history the same cycle repeats itself; so let the people remember, let them learn and let them hear the warning voice of God.

Sometimes the past speaks with a voice of hope. No book in the Old Testament so clearly shows the activity of God in history as does the second part of the Book of *Isaiah*. It was written to put new heart into a people so humiliated by years of exile that they felt themselves forsaken by God. "Why do you say, O Jacob, and speak, O Israel, 'My way is hid from the Lord, and my right is disregarded by my God?' . . . Look to the rock from which you were hewn, and to the quarry from which you were digged". That rock, that quarry is the history of all that God has done for the generations before them; and what God has done once he can do again. Israel's future will not be decided by what seems to be the indifference of God in the present; rather it will be decided in the light of those mighty acts of deliverance by which God has vindicated his holy name in the past.

Only a dullard finds history dull. The historian, if he be a philosopher or a man of faith, can read it as an exciting story with a continuous plot and in each period of the past he can see the significance for the present. When someone asked Professor Charles Beard what lessons he had learned from a lifetime of studying history, he specified four: "First, whom the gods would destroy they make mad with power; second, the mills of God grind slowly, yet they grind exceeding small; third, the bee fertilizes the flower it robs; fourth, when it is dark enough you see the stars." In that point of view history is not just a chronicle of events and dates; it is the story of God with man and man with God. Through the events of the past God speaks to the present with a voice of warning and hope, and his voice is very powerful.

The Bible tells us that we can hear the voice of the Lord

speaking through prophecy. The Epistle to the Hebrews begins, "In many and various ways God spoke of old to our fathers by the prophets . . ." That is what the prophets were—not clairvoyants or fortune tellers but spokesmen for God. They were men whom God designated, men who felt called by God and who lived so close to God that they could think his thoughts after him and speak to the individual and society on behalf of God. They prefaced their prophecies with, "Thus says the Lord," then proclaimed not their own words but the Word which God had given them to proclaim.

In Sunday worship it is usual to preface the reading of Holy Scripture by saying, "Let us hear the Word of God." Because the Bible contains the sermons of the great prophets and all the sacred writings of God's people, we believe that God speaks to us through the Bible in a way that is true of no other collection of writings in the world's literature. God speaks *through* the Bible. This written record of the past is not itself the Word of God; it becomes the Word of God when God uses it as a means of his living encounter with us in the present. This happens when we read the Bible through the eyes of faith and recognize our own situation in its pages. Then the Bible becomes the voice of God speaking to our situation and it is a voice very powerful.

The late Bishop Berggrav of Norway wrote an article in which he said that, though he had always read the Bible, it was not until the war years, when all else had failed and he turned to Scripture with a desperate faith, that he really discovered it to be the Word of God. During his arrest and trial and three years in a Nazi prison the Bible became the voice of God speaking to his soul. He admits that sometimes the voice failed to speak, and he felt alone, forsaken. In such a black mood one day he got the idea to read aloud. At first nothing happened, but an hour later he noticed how his mood had changed. Confidence had returned. Again God had spoken to his weak son. "Why aloud?" asks Bishop Berggrav. "I don't know," he replies, "but I think the sound of the voice was like the incarnation of the printed word and that I had physically acted in faith."

The Bible tells us that we can hear the voice of the Lord *speaking through conscience.* God spoke that way to Elijah.

Forsaken, despised, hunted like a beast of prey, the Hebrew prophet fled into the wilderness, crawled into a cave and prayed that he might die, but God tracked him down and asked, "What are you doing here, Elijah?" Out came the bitter complaint of Israel's apostasy and her murder of God's messengers, "I, even I only, am left; and they seek my life, to take it away." God did not coddle this man's self-pity. He said, "Go forth, and stand upon the mount before the Lord." As Elijah stood there, a hurricane pulverized the rocks before him, then an earthquake tore open the ground, then a fire decimated the forest, but these cataclysms of nature communicated no truth to him. Then in his own conscience he heard a still, small voice saying, in effect, "Come off it, Elijah. You needn't be solicitous for God. You know that he has the situation in hand. Stop feeling sorry for yourself and go back to the work he has given you to do."

The still, small voice may speak to us even while we sleep. That was how God spoke to Joseph, the human parent of Jesus. In a dream an angel told him not to be afraid to marry the pregnant Mary; in a second dream he was warned to escape the madness of King Herod by taking his wife and child to Egypt; in another dream he received word that it was safe for them to return to the land of Israel. Dreams may be explained as the release of the subconscious mind, but that is all the more reason for believing that God uses them as a means of speaking to us. Our conscious minds may be so preoccupied with the day's business that God can get through to us only while we sleep. Another Psalmist saw deeply into human nature when he wrote that God "gives to his beloved in sleep".

The still, small voice may speak in a sudden flash of intuition. Every man who lives close to God can recall an experience where his reason and the advice of friends pointed him in one direction but where an irresistible inner impulse drove him in the opposite direction. Psychologists call this auto-suggestion— which seems a very good explanation of the way that God communicates his purpose for our lives. God thinks through us, not for us. He does not insult our faculties; he uses our faculties. He makes us sensitive to his will and his laws, and it is often this spiritual sensitivity that guides us and prevails over our natural desires. In George Bernard Shaw's *St. Joan*, when the Bishop tells Joan of Arc that the voices which she hears are only in her imagination, she replies, "How else does God speak except through the imagination?" God does speak through the imagination, through the conscious or unconscious mind, and his voice is very powerful.

The Bible tells us that we can hear the voice of the Lord *speaking in Jesus Christ*. That was certainly the conviction of people who knew the historic Jesus. On one occasion four friends made an opening in the roof and lowered a paralyzed man at Jesus' feet. Seeing their faith, he said to the paralytic, "My son, your sins are forgiven." That scandalized the Pharisees. "It is blasphemy!" they exploded. "Who can forgive sins but God alone?" They were right, of course. Only God *can* forgive sins, but what God alone can do Jesus *did* there and then. As proof that he could forgive sins he cured the paralytic with the words "I say to you, rise, take up your pallet and go home", words so filled with healing power that many of the spectators knew that they had been listening to the voice of God.

That voice spoke in many tones. Sometimes it was compassionate, as when Jesus said to a woman caught in the act of adultery, "Neither do I condemn thee: go, and sin no more." Sometimes he spoke sternly as he did to Peter when that loyal disciple tempted him to evade the cross, "Get behind me, Satan! For you are not on the side of God, but of men". Sometimes it was a pleading voice, "Come unto me, all ye that labour and are heavy laden, and I will give you rest." Sometimes a commanding voice, as when he silenced the storm, "Peace! Be still!"; and drove out a demon, "You dumb and deaf spirit, I command you, come out of him, and never enter him again!" God speaks as Jesus spoke—in compassionate, stern, pleading, commanding tones; always with a voice very powerful.

The New Testament has not said everything about Jesus when it says that he spoke with the voice of God. As the first apostles looked back in the light of their companionship with the risen Christ, they made a more daring affirmation. They said that Jesus *was* the voice of God. Writes the author of Hebrews: "In many and various ways God spoke of old to our fathers by the prophets; but in these last days he has spoken to us by a Son". John, the beloved disciple, wrote even more profoundly of his Lord: "In the beginning was the Word, and the Word was with God, and the Word was God . . . And the Word became flesh and dwelt among us, full of grace and truth . . ." That voice of God which said at Creation, "Let there be light!" which divided the waters of the Red Sea, which spoke through the mouths of the prophets and which whispers in the conscience of man—that eternal voice of God became not only audible but visible in Jesus Christ and once and for all declared itself in a language that all men can understand.

One of the beautiful Bible stories that we learned in childhood is the story of the infant Samuel, but it was not written in the first place as a children's story. See how it begins: "And the word of the Lord was rare in those days; there was no frequent vision." Not for spiritually sensitive children but for hard-boiled, materialistic grown-ups the Bible tells of the little lad in the temple courts who heard a voice while he slept and, learning from the old priest Eli that it was the voice of God, responded obediently, "Speak, Lord, for thy servant hears." This is God's Word to our spiritually deaf generation; it could be God's Word to you. Next time you gaze upon nature's grandeur, or recall the events of history, or read the Bible, or commune with your own heart, or come up to the Sacrament of Christ's body and blood, let this be your prayer, "Speak, Lord, for thy servant hears." It may be that God will speak to *you*, and the voice of the Lord will be very powerful.

GOD LAUGHS

What troubles me about a lot of the "new theology" being preached in the churches today is that it depersonalizes God. He whom I once called "Heavenly Father" has been turned into a vague, oblong blur. It almost persuades me to be an atheist. I cannot be interested in such a God, because it seems that he is not interested in me. I cannot pray to this God or have fellowship with him; and going to Church seems as impersonal as shopping in a super-market after I have been accustomed to friendly personal attention at the corner grocery store.

I mourn the death of the God who-used-to-be. I thought of him not as a Person but as personal, possessing intelligence and emotions, holding purposes and preferences, of which our human nature is a tiny, imperfect reflection. This was a God who entered human experience and dealt with men, wrestling with them as he wrestled with Jacob, tracking them down as he tracked down Jonah. This was the God of the Bible, the God of Abraham, Isaac and Jacob, the God and Father of our Lord Jesus Christ. He had strong feelings—anger that could be aroused, compassion for human weakness and sorrow and suffering.

Take this verse from the *37th Psalm: "The Lord shall laugh at him . . ."* Nothing is more personal than laughter. Have you ever thought of God laughing? The thought is not irreverent if we can believe that God is like Jesus. I often picture Jesus and his disciples having a good laugh together and I often think there must be laughter in heaven. So writes another Psalmist: "He that sitteth in the heavens shall laugh." The personal God has a sense of humour; there must be some things that he finds funny, even the things that he himself created. Here is a poem that suggests it:

When God had finished the stars and whirl of coloured suns
He turned His mind from big things to fashion little ones,
Beautiful tiny things (like daises) He made, and then

He made the comical ones in case the minds of men
  Should stiffen and become
  Dull, humourless and glum:
And so forgetful of their Maker be
As to take even themselves—*quite seriously*.
Caterpillars and cats are lively and excellent puns:
All God's jokes are good—even the practical ones!
And as for the duck, I think God must have smiled a bit
Seeing those bright eyes blink on the day He fashioned it.
And He's probably laughing still at the sound that came out
    of its bill!"[1]

Laughter expresses many moods. There is the lyrical laughter of sheer joy, the hollow laughter of cynicism, the brutal laughter that cruel men hurled at Jesus on his Cross. Then there is the derisive, scornful laugh of the man who laughs last. This is what the Psalmist writes about when he says, "The Lord shall laugh at him . . ." It is a way of emphasizing one of the great truths in the Bible, the truth of God's justice. The God of this man's experience is *a God who laughs*. God, he declares, will always have the last laugh. Wrestling with the age-old question, "Does it pay to be good?" the Hebrew poet answers confidently, "Yes, it does pay. It pays to be good for a laugh, God's laugh".

This question still vexes the human spirit—Does it pay to be good? Despite the insights of the men who wrote the Bible, many people feel tempted to answer with a resounding "No!" They see the glaring inequalities of life, the success of sinners and the suffering of saints, and they exclaim bitterly, "Virtue obviously has no reward and vice no punishment. It makes no difference how you live. It does not pay to be good."

Doesn't life prove it? I know a woman who has turned sour because her husband does not make very much money and she cannot keep up with their more affluent friends. What galls her is that once she could keep up with the best of them. Her husband used to be the sales manager in a large private corporation. He drew a big salary, and they lived in a big house. One day the president of the company asked him to endorse certain household appliances that were not new but were defective

[1] DUCKS: III by Frederick W. Harvey in *The Questing Spirit*, Ed. Halford E. Luccock and Frances Brentano (Coward-McCann, New York), pp. 412–13.

products rebuilt and being sold as new products. The sales manager protested, "This is dishonest! I can't do it!" "Well, you had better do it", warned his employer, "if you want to keep your job." So now he draws a small salary and lives in a small house, and his wife is bitter about it. She doesn't think that it pays to be good.

That is what bothered the Hebrew poet, and to deal with his problem he put his thoughts into writing. His poem is not the greatest in the Bible nor is it the most sophisticated treatment of this particular problem. The authors of *Job* and *Psalm 73* found a more mature solution, but this man had at least the advantage of speaking out of a lifetime of personal experience. His own words, "*I have been young, and now am old*," suggest that he wrote with the wisdom that belongs to old age.

He begins with a piece of homely advice—which by itself does not necessarily lend weight to the Psalm. Advice is cheap, and most of us, as we grow older, dispense it more freely, especially if we have not been guided by it ourselves. But this man is worth listening to because evidently he practised what he preached. He says, in effect, "When you see crooks and scoundrels enjoying more than their fair share of the good things of life, don't be jealous of them, don't get all hot and bothered and don't make it your excuse to imitate them and do something stupid." Many people do exactly that. Convinced that there is no justice in the world, they exclaim, "Oh, what the hell!" and promptly lapse into licence, dishonesty or infidelity. "Why shouldn't I let the producers make love to me?" cried the young actress. "The others do, and they are happier and more successful than I am. Sure, I have ideals, but they don't get me anywhere".

The Psalmist speaks to the young lady and others like her and he counsels a more serene, philosophical attitude: "*Fret not thyself because of evildoers, neither be thou envious against the workers of iniquity.*" He adds, "*Cease from anger, and forsake wrath: fret not thyself in any wise to do evil.*" Behind his homely advice lies deep religious conviction which has grown out of a lifetime of experience with God. The Psalmist has lived close to God for many years and reached the conclusion that, whatever else he may be, he is a just God. His justice controls all of life, so that the world is like a responsible and well-ordered society. Crime continues to flourish, and for a time criminals seem to get away with their crimes, but life has a nemesis for every sin, and sooner or later justice catches up with them. Men may flout God's laws, they may even laugh at the silly idea of his justice, but let them remember that he laughs loudest who laughs last, and in God's world God will always have the last laugh.

The Hebrew poet knew what he was talking about because apparently he had lived long enough to see with his own eyes the outworking of God's justice. Most of us are not that fortunate. God does not pay his accounts at the end of each week. He does not always pay them within our orbit of experience or even within our lifetime. We must live by faith, not by sight. We can only take the Psalmist at his word when he writes of evildoers, "*For they shall soon be cut down like the grass, and wither as the green herb . . . Their sword shall enter into their own heart, and their bows shall be broken.*" It is a hopeful view of life, less vindictive than comforting. We might put it down to wishful thinking except that we keep coming up against the fact that the Psalmist is not theorizing but writing out of his own experience. His most memorable and picturesque figure of speech takes the form of a personal testimony: "*I have seen the wicked in great power, and spreading himself like a green bay tree. Yet he passed away, and, lo, he was not: yea, I sought him, but he could not be found.*"

This could be a philosophy of history; it could be the story of many dictators. Suppose that Rip Van Winkle had lived in Germany in the 1930s and had seen Hitler rising to power, spreading himself like a green bay tree and enslaving the small nations beneath his shadow. It would be a time of terror, as indeed it was a time of terror; so one day the sensitive Rip Van Winkle climbs a high mountain to get away from the chaos in the valley and to see life in a longer perspective. There he falls asleep and remains asleep for twenty years, oblivious to the horror and the suffering and the revolutionary changes caused by the Second World War. He descends the mountain in the 1950s and is confused and bewildered by all the changes about him—a vacant lot where his house once stood, a prison reduced to bombed-out rubble, a different flag flying over the city hall. Where are the Brown Shirts, the Gestapo, the concentration camps? Where are the armies of the Third Reich? Where is Hitler himself? The destroyer has been destroyed;

and Rip Van Winkle, whether he is a religious man or not, can echo the Psalmist: "I have seen the wicked in great power, and spreading himself like a green bay tree. Yet he passed away, and, lo, he was not: yea, I sought him, but he could not be found."

Sometimes the justice of God does operate most dramatically within a single lifetime. Years ago a real estate agent on the west coast of the United States had a pamphlet printed which he sent to every American millionaire. (Needless to say, my copy did not come to me directly.) The pamphlet carried a story which was so fantastic that it has to be true. It seems that in 1923 eight of the world's most successful men met at the Edgewater Beach Hotel in Chicago. Present were: the president of the world's largest independent steel company; the president of the world's largest utility company; the greatest wheat speculator in the United States; the president of the New York Stock Exchange; a member of the Federal Cabinet; the greatest financier in the history of Wall Street; the president of the Bank of International Settlements; the head of the world's largest monopoly. Collectively these men controlled more wealth than there was in the United States Treasury. For years the newspapers had featured their success stories and held them up as examples to the youth of the nation. Look at their story twenty-five years later. The president of the world's largest independent steel company, Charles M. Schwab, lived on borrowed money for the last five years of his life and died penniless. The head of the world's largest utility company, Samuel Insull, died in obscurity in Canada. The greatest wheat speculator in the United States, Arthur Cutten, died abroad, insolvent. The president of the New York Stock Exchange, Richard Whitney, served a term in Sing Sing. The member of the Federal Cabinet, Albert Fall, was released from prison so that he could die at home. The greatest financier on Wall Street, Jesse Livermore, committed suicide. The president of the Bank of International Settlements, Leon Frazer, committed suicide. The head of the world's largest monopoly, Ivar Kreuger, the so-called "Match King", leaped from a plane crossing the English Channel and committed suicide.

In terms of real life that is what the Psalmist means when he says of the evildoer, "The Lord shall laugh at him . . ." Evil men do seem to prosper, but evil, no matter how successful it appears in terms of wealth and power, is still evil at all times, in all places and in all people. Moreoever, the moral order of God will have the last word on the evildoer, and it will be a full answer given in God's own way and time. In God's world God will always have the last laugh. We have to believe *that*, or else life in this world becomes senseless and intolerable. It becomes a colossal joke—and whose joke?

Now the Psalmist turns to write about the reward of the righteous man. He does not go so far as to say that it pays to be good, because, if that were the case, virtue would be prudential rather than moral, and goodness would be a kind of cosmic insurance policy taken out by calculating, cold-blooded moralists to save their own skins. The Psalmist, however, does give some rather convincing reasons for goodness. He says that the righteous man with his poverty is really better off than the wicked man with his wealth. Why? Because God likes the righteous man and gives him inward resources that he does not give to the evildoer. These resources show themselves in a time of collective tragedy. The righteous "*shall not be ashamed in the evil time: and in the days of famine they shall be satisfied.*" Because he is human and not divine, the righteous man will fall sometimes but "*he shall not be utterly cast down: for the Lord upholdeth him with his hand.*" When tragedy strips wicked men of worldly wealth, they have nothing to fall back on; they are helpless. "*But the salvation of the righteous is of the Lord: he is their strength in the time of trouble.*" Again what gives weight to this hopeful view of life and makes it more than wishful thinking is the fact that the Psalmist writes out of his own experience. Again his most unforgettable statement takes the form of personal testimony: "*I have been young, and now am old; yet have I not seen the righteous forsaken, nor his seed begging bread.*"

But is it really true? Does it actually work out in terms of real life that "*A little that a righteous man hath is better than the riches of many wicked*"? Is a good man who makes two thousand dollars a year better off than a bad man who makes two hundred thousand dollars. The Psalmist comes close to the heart of the matter by referring constantly to a man's "seed", his children and grandchildren who are, after all, life's greatest treasure. Their love and loyalty become increasingly precious to a man, especially as he grows older. Without his children's affection all the money in the world is worthless. Given the affection of his children, he does not complain about other privations. But love, loyalty, respect and affection are the rewards of goodness. Our sons and daughters take their cue from us; they become what we consciously and unconsciously make of them. The brittle, callous woman, who will hurt anyone to get what she wants, has no cause to complain if her equally brittle and callous daughter ignores and despises her in her old age. Honest, upright, God-fearing parents, whose successful son visits them faithfully and provides lovingly for their needs, are simply seeing in his life a goodness which is a reflection of their own.

Harry Emerson Fosdick tells of a woman who, comparatively young, was left a widow with five children. By careful management she saw all of them through school and college. One son became president of a great railway system, another became president of a university, another became a leading pioneer in his field of medical research. That woman was an extraordinary personality. She died in her ninety-sixth year, and on the day of her funeral the children said that they had never seen her impatient or distraught to the point of giving up, even in the most troubled times. It was the university president who declared that no one could understand his mother who did not understand the meaning of faith. Her faith, he said, was a force that released radiance and power.[1] Looking at this woman and her remarkable family, one might say with the Psalmist, "I have been young, and now am old; yet have I not seen the righteous forsaken, nor his seed begging bread."

Now the Psalmist makes his greatest affirmation of faith, so great that Jesus echoed it in the Beatitudes: "*The meek shall inherit the earth; and shall delight themselves in the abundance of peace.*" This is the final answer to the question, Does it pay to be good? The Psalmist says, in effect, "Some day, in God's righteous order, only the good men will survive."

"The meek shall inherit the earth"—It would sound ridiculous, even coming from Jesus, and we should certainly doubt its truth if his own life had not proved it to be true. We listen to him, however, because he was the meekest of

---

[1] Harry Emerson Fosdick, *Riverside Sermons* (Harper and Brothers, New York, 1958), p. 113.

men, meek in the sense that his strength was restrained and gentle. He who could have entered the world as royalty came as a Baby in a barn. He who could have commanded a conquering army rode into the city on the back of a borrowed donkey. He who could have crushed men into submission appealed to them with words of sweet reasonableness and loving acts of mercy. He who could have destroyed his enemies with a single stroke allowed them to lead him like a lamb to the slaughter. Yet who has inherited the earth—Christ or his enemies? Who alone has continued his triumphant march through the centuries while kingdoms, empires, thrones, and dictators have risen and fallen again into the dust of oblivion?

> I saw the Conquerers riding by
> > With cruel lips and faces wan:
> Musing on kingdoms sacked and burned
> > There rode the Mongol Genghis Khan;
>
> And Alexander, like a god,
> > Who sought to weld the world in one;
> And Caesar with his laurel wreath;
> > And like a thing from Hell, the Hun;
>
> And leading, like a star the van,
> > Heedless of upstretched arm and groan,
> Inscrutable Napoleon went
> > Dreaming of empire, and alone . . .
>
> Then all they perished from the earth
> > As fleeting shadows from a glass,
> And, conquering down the centuries,
> > Came Christ, the Swordless, on an ass!"[1]

Jesus of Nazareth is history's supreme vindication of a Hebrew Psalmist who once dared to predict that "the meek shall inherit the earth". Because of Jesus, the most righteous man who ever lived, crucified by the ultimate concentration of human wickedness, and raised from the dead to the throne of the universe, we can believe that in God's world it does pay to be good. It pays to be good for a laugh, God's laugh.

[1] "The Conquerers" by Harry Kemp in *Masterpieces of Religious Verse*, Ed. James Dalton Morrison (Harper and Row, New York and London, 1948), p. 210.

Because of Jesus we need not get excited over the apparent unequalities of life. We can heed the counsel of this ancient wise man who said,

"*Trust in the Lord, and do good; so shalt thou dwell in the land, and verily thou shalt be fed.*

Delight thyself also in the Lord; and he shall give thee the desires of thine heart.

Commit thy way unto the Lord; trust also in him; and he shall bring it to pass . . .

Rest in the Lord, and wait patiently for him . . ."

GOD CHASTENS

A modern novel that packs a powerful psychological punch is Nevil Shute's *The Breaking Wave*, also published under the title, *Requiem for a Wren*. It tells the sad story of Janet Prentice, a refined and capable English girl who joined the Wrens during the Second World War. She surprised the navy men by her ability to handle an anti-aircraft gun and even won the praise of the First Sea Lord for her skill in target practice. On April 29, 1944 the guns opened fire on a Junkers aircraft which was flying low over the Solent and which everyone assumed to be an enemy reconnaissance plane taking photographs. Janet scored a direct hit. The plane burst into flames and crashed. When they searched the wreckage they found the charred bodies of seven *Luftwaffe* sergeants.

That evening Janet was summoned to the captain's quarters where an R.A.F. intelligence officer inquired if she had not noticed that the aircraft was flying with its wheels down. If this had been the case, it meant that the crew wanted to land and surrender. Everything pointed to the fact that the seven airmen were not the enemy but were Poles or Czechs dressed in German uniforms and attempting to escape from Germany. At first Janet was numbed by the enormity of her ghastly mistake. Her numbness gradually gave way to a burning sensation of guilt that would not let her eat and filled her drugged sleep with hideous nightmares.

Seven days later her fiancé, a young Australian serving as a frogman with the British Navy, was killed trying to disconnect mines off the coast of France. Janet received the news with no outward emotion. She had been waiting for it; she accepted it as the judgment of God. A month later came the D-Day invasion and with it the news that the motor transport ship bearing her father had been struck and sunk in error by allied shells. Still Janet remained stoically silent. Now she was quite convinced that God was punishing her. She seemed to have no feelings at all except towards the little dog which had belonged to her fiancé. When a Sherman tank ran over the animal and crushed it, Janet's pent-up emotions exploded, and she went to pieces, because now it appeared certain to her that she would have to pay the full price for her terrible mistake. Every one of the seven lives she had taken must be atoned for. The Celestial Huntsman would fire seven arrows at her, each one striking deeper, and the last one wounding her mortally. There could be no escaping God's dreadful judgment, nor did she want to escape it.

Discharged from the Wrens on medical grounds, Janet returned to her home in Oxford. When her mother died, she resigned herself to the inevitable. Three arrows left. Now she had nowhere to go and nothing to do but wait. She tried to work, she drifted around England, then she travelled abroad to Seattle to care for a sick aunt, hoping that it might restore some meaning to her empty life. Again she found an object of affection in her aunt's dog; again the animal was killed. When her aunt died, she knew that only one arrow remained and that it was obviously intended for her. She had been carefully saving some of her aunt's heavy pain-killing drugs. Should she now take an overdose and put an end to it all? Thoughts of suicide drove her to consult a doctor to whom she confided her whole story and her certainty that in suffering so many bereavements she was expiating her sins. The doctor gave his opinion that the expiation angle was "all baloney" and advised her to go to Australia and try to make contact with her fiance's parents who didn't even know of her existence.

Janet followed the doctor's advice and arrived at the Australian sheep farm under an assumed name where she took a position as a house maid. For a few months she lived in blissful happiness with these wonderfully kind people, never revealing her identity but daring to believe that there might be at least a limited future for her in serving the parents of the man whom she had loved. Then came word that her fiancé's brother, who had met her in England during the war, was coming home to settle in Australia and help his father run the sheep farm. Janet did not have the courage to face him, nor did she have the strength to leave. After making the last entry in her diary she measured out a lethal dose of drugs and sank into the sleep of death, believing that her seven-fold debt to God had been paid in full.

Whatever else you may call her, you cannot call Janet Prentice insane. Her conviction that the rapid succession of personal tragedies did not happen by chance but were God's judgment on the tragedy which she had needlessly caused is a conviction solidly rooted in the theology of the Old Testament. The Jews connected all tragedy with wrong-doing. They argued inexorably that, if a man suffered, he was paying the price for his sins, Recall how monotonously Job's "comforters" pressed that point. "Who ever perished, being innocent?" they callously argued. The rabbis declared categorically, "There is no death without sin, and no pains without some transgression". Even the disciples of Jesus, their minds conditioned by Old Testament theology, asked him concerning a blind man, "Rabbi, who sinned, this man or his parents, that he was born blind?" Jesus himself, not because he believed this crude theology but because he knew that the patient believed it, cured a paralyzed man by the strange expedient of saying to him, "My son, your sins are forgiven." So Janet Prentice, evidently a religious girl whose thinking was also conditioned by the Old Testament, had plenty of support for supposing that God in his judgment of man operates on the strict principle of "an eye for an eye, and a tooth for a tooth". Seven sins; seven arrows—it was as logical as that.

But wait a moment before you agree with the doctor who told Janet that the expiation angle was "all baloney". Granted we find repulsive the image of God as a Celestial Huntsman fitting arrows to his bow and standing poised to shoot them into the hearts of men according to the number of their sins, do we not find equally repulsive the image of God as "a good guy upstairs" who insults us by acting as though he did not notice our sins, let alone treat them seriously? How could we ever respect a God who administered his world with less regard for crime and punishment than we humans have in the administration of our earthly societies? The Bible simply seeks to establish that we live not in a jungle but in a moral order governed by God's laws which carry their own retribution when we violate them, and this is what the Bible means when it uses that awesome phrase, "the wrath of God". God's wrath is not an emotion such as we feel when we become angry; it is a principle of justice that stands like a stone wall and bruises the body and soul of every man who tries to break it down.

The Bible speaks about "the wrath of God" only because some of the men who wrote the Bible experienced God's wrath as a very real fact in their lives. One of them was the writer of the *38th Psalm*. Like Janet Prentice this Hebrew poet suffered a succession of personal tragedies, so acute and so closely-related that he sees them not as mere chance but as the chastening activity of God. He believes that the God of man's experience is *a God who chastens*. Hear how he cries to God: "*O Lord, rebuke me not in thy wrath: neither chasten me in thy hot displeasure.*" It is he who coins the archery image and speaks of God's justice in terms of a series of arrows aimed at him from heaven. Listen to his complaint: "*For thine arrows stick fast in me, and thy hand presseth me sore.*" The Psalmist tells us what some of those arrows were.

First, a pathological sense of guilt. I say "pathological" to distinguish it from the healthy emotion of guilt which is a normal reaction to our own mistakes and negligence and which usually stimulates us to do something constructive about them. But there was nothing healthy about the guilt of the Psalmist which made him cry out, "*For mine iniquities are gone over mine head: as an heavy burden they are too heavy for me.*" We have no idea what the Psalmist had done to deserve his emotional misery. Perhaps nothing at all; perhaps some foolish, impulsive blunder, hastily committed and at once regretted. Whatever it was, the memory of it engulfed his conscience like swirling flood-waters and weighed on his soul like a back-breaking burden.

You hear it said that guilt is no longer a problem with most people. This may be true of the man who has no conscience, but in civilized society where shall we find such a man? Most of us, as a result of character-training in home, school, church and community, have developed a moral nervous system which reacts to our own wrong-doing, or even to the suggestion of wrong-doing, as sensitively the body nerves react to a red-hot poker. We can treat the conscience like a barking dog, tell it to lie down and be quiet, but it only slinks into the corner of our subconscious minds and gathers strength to bark louder later on. Many a person, suffering from emotional disturbance in middle-age, has been analyzed only to find his illness rooted in forgotten adventures which at the time he could not square with his own conscience. No man with any moral sense can permanently suppress the memory of his moral mistakes. Something will bring it to the surface. Even in his dreams it will rise up to haunt him, as the faces of those dead airmen haunted Janet Prentice; and, if he is a religious man, he may accept his emotional misery as the judgment of God.

When guilt becomes too heavy, the conscience may ask the mind to bear part of the burden, and the result can be severe mental strain often leading to breakdown. This is the point where guilt becomes an obsession. A man thinks of the wrong that he has done and he can think of nothing else. The thought of his dreadful mistake hangs over his world like a dark cloud, shutting out the sunlight, so that everything appears drab and ugly. This was another of God's arrows that pierced the Psalmist: "*I am troubled; I am bowed down greatly; I go mourning all the day long.*"

That was Janet Prentice's condition. In the days following the aeroplane crash it worried her friends that she seemed to go to about her duties as if nothing had happened, but those who knew her well could imagine the accumulating guilt that must be dammed up inside her. When the dam burst, she had to be placed in a hospital under psychiatric care. She seemed normal at the time of her discharge but she was never herself again. She drifted from one job to another, unable to concentrate upon work of any sort, because she was too preoccupied with her guilt; it dominated her mind. She was troubled, she was bowed down greatly, she went mourning all the day long. Then her mind began playing tricks on her. Unable to think logically, she reached the irrational conclusion not only that God intended to punish her but that she had to be punished and that she wanted to be punished. That is what obsessional guilt can do to a morally sensitive person.

When guilt becomes too heavy even for the mind, the body is asked to bear the burden. The guilty person becomes physically ill and, if he is a religious man, this is where he really begins to imagine that God is punishing him. There can be no mistaking that the writer of the 38th Psalm was physically unwell. He suffered in his body like a wounded soldier who had, in fact, been riddled with arrows from the bow of an enemy and left to die. You can sense the pain and the self-condemnation out of which he prays to God: "*There is no soundness in my flesh because of thine anger; neither is there any rest in my bones because of my sin . . . My wounds stink and are corrupt because of my foolishness . . . For my loins are filled with a loathsome disease . . . My heart panteth, my strength faileth me: as for the light of mine eyes, it also is gone from me . . ."*

There was nothing unique about this man's condition or about his state of mind concerning it. Nor was there anything unique about the paralytic in the Gospel story whom Jesus healed by saying "your sins are forgiven." The sense of sin, when it becomes too acute, can induce paralysis. Whoever denies the possibility of an organic relationship between illness and guilt has simply not kept abreast of the developments in modern medicine. Medical journals abound in case-histories of physical sufferings which had their roots in some spiritual cause, and foremost among these spiritual causes was the sense of shame over wrong-doing. One eminent physician states his conviction as the result of treating many patients, "Most of the causes of mental derangement of the functional type are due to a sense of guilt." An unusual little book on the teaching of the Bible in relation to health has been written by S. I. McMillen, M.D. under the title, *None of these Diseases*.[1] The author deals with a number of common illnesses—peptic ulcers, migraine headaches, high blood pressure, nervous exhaustion, etc.—and in each case holds the patient himself responsible for his condition on the grounds that he failed to live by the laws of God. If he had obeyed the laws of God he would have suffered "none of these diseases". They might be the simple laws of health and hygiene or they might be the great moral laws which, if we break them, engender within us such a pathological sense of guilt that it makes us physically ill.

The Psalmist felt terribly forsaken in his illness of mind and body and he accepted this loneliness as another of God's arrows. "*My lovers and my friends stand aloof from my sore; and my kinsmen stand afar off.*" This may actually happen. When a person has, in fact, done something dreadfully wrong and is paying up for his mistake, his friends and even his own family, who judge less mercifully than God, may find him an embarrassment and go out of their way to avoid him. So it happened to Job. No one was ever more forsaken than this solitary sufferer sitting alone on a dung heap and scraping

[1] Oliphants.

his boils. Only three of his former friends came to comfort him, and their comfort soon turned to a most uncomfortable self-righteous judgment. Or it may simply seem that way. The guilty person may be so obsessed with his guilt that he feels ashamed to face people, so he deliberately withdraws into a shell of isolation and becomes incapable of all the normal relationships. That is what happened to Janet Prentice. After her mother's death she sold the house, moved away from Oxford, left no forwarding address and cut off all her former friendships. The sense of guilt carries with it a terrible sense of aloneness.

This loneliness can develop into a persecution complex as it did with the Old Testament Psalmist. His enemies may have been real enough, but his description of their malevolence could suggest an over-active imagination. At any rate, their enmity struck like another arrow in his flesh. To God he cries out, "*They also that seek after my life lay snares for me: and they that seek my hurt speak mischievous things, and imagine deceits all the day long.*" At no time did Janet Prentice sink to this low level of imagination, but it does happen to people when they are sick in mind and body and convinced that God is punishing them for their sins. The guilty person begins to imagine that the whole human race is ganged up in a conspiracy against him. He goes around looking for slights and insults. Every word that people speak, every gesture that they make he interprets as a snide reference to the thing that fills his mind with guilt. I read of one woman who was so obsessed with her own sense of guilt that she could not go to the theatre because she felt sure that the playwright had known her story and woven it into his play. She could not listen to the radio because it seemed to her that even the popular songs had to do with her life's tragedy. She stopped going to church because every sermon seemed to be an exposé of her particular sin. She believed that people who sat in a restaurant and rode in the bus were nudging one another and whispering about her, even though they were total strangers. This poor woman's sense of guilt had created within her a persecution complex.

From a purely academic standpoint—if you *can* read it academically and not identify yourself with the author—the 38th Psalm is an absorbing study of the anatomy of guilt. A man does something which he knows to be wrong, perhaps intentionally, perhaps mistakenly as Janet Prentice did when her eagerness to fire the anti-aircraft gun blinded her to the nature of the target. First, a sense of shame stabs his conscience. Then, as he becomes obsessed with the image of what he has done, it begins to play havoc with his mind. The mind passes part of the burden to the body, and the body becomes organically ill. Sick in mind and body, the guilty person builds a wall around himself, shutting out his friends and imagining that all who want to penetrate that wall are his enemies. When the shame, the suffering, the loneliness become too acute, and he feels that he cannot stand it much longer, the guilty person becomes depressed and desperate, and thoughts of suicide may enter his mind. If he is a religious man he may even convince himself, as Janet Prentice convinced herself, that this is the honourable thing to do, the heroic acceptance of God's final arrow, the ultimate expiation for his sin.

To the problem of guilt the unreligious man has a very obvious solution. He simply suggests that we leave God out of the picture altogether, and his solution might be useful except for one thing—it doesn't work. True, Janet Prentice interpreted her succession of tragedies as God's judgment on her disastrous mistake, but the tragedies would have happened anyway, so how was she to deal with them? True, the Old Testament Psalmist saw his series of sufferings as God's chastening for his sins, but he would have suffered anyway, so how was he to deal with it? To repudiate God does not help us when we have to pay the price for our moral blunders; rather it deprives us of our greatest source of comfort and hope. "It is a fearful thing," says the *Epistle to the Hebrews*, "to fall into the hands of the living God." But surely the most fearful thing in life would be to fall out of the hands of the living God and be left to oneself in a world where moral mistakes bring their own moral retribution. There is, after all, a worse fate than God's judgment, and that is that God should cease to judge us, should ignore us and cast us off. Let us not be afraid to speak of the wrath of God. We can speak of it with tenderness, because even as wrath it is still grace, an evidence that God is still interested in us, that he still cares what happens to us and still loves us.

Besides, a new possibility comes into view when we connect some of our sufferings with our sins and interpret them as the chastening activity of God. It is the possibility that God in his

love will come where we are and will do something to save us
even from the outworking of his own justice. This is what the
Psalmist prayed for. This was his hope: "*Forsake me not, O
Lord: O my God, be not far from me. Make haste to help me,
O Lord my salvation.*" With us it is more than a possibility,
more than a hope. We know that God has answered the
Psalmist's prayer. We know that in a way which avails for all
men at all times God has once and for all entered our human
experience and on the Cross of Jesus Christ acted to save us
from his own chastening wrath.

GOD SECURES

In Dostoevsky's *Crime and Punishment* there is a poignant dialogue between the murderer, Raskolnikov, and Sonia, a girl who befriends him. Sonia, a religious girl, has turned prostitute in order to support her impoverished family. Her one prayer is that the same fate shall not befall her little sister, Polenka; but Raskolnikov, tortured by guilt, taunts her cruelly. The conversation goes like this:

" 'It will be the same with Polenka, no doubt,' he said suddenly.

'No, no! It can't be, no!' Sonia cried aloud in desperation, as though she had been stabbed. 'God would not allow anything so awful!'

'He lets others come to it.'

'No, no! God will protect her, God!' she repeated beside herself.

'But, perhaps, there is no God at all,' Raskolnikov answered with a sort of malignance, laughed and looked at her.

Sonia's face suddenly changed; a tremor passed over it. She looked at him with unutterable reproach, tried to say something, but could not speak and broke into bitter, bitter sobs, hiding her face in her hands."

I often ask myself if the clever intellectuals, who confidently declare "the Death of God", feel any sense of shame as they listen to the sobbing of simple believers. A man takes on a terrible responsibility when he kicks the foundations from beneath the faith of another man. Sonia had nothing decent in life but religion. God was the one certainty to which she could cling, her only source of hope and comfort and security. It was cruel of Raskolnikov to take God away from her, not only cruel but unnecessary. He had only the support of his own doubt to declare harshly, "Perhaps there is no God at all." He would have had the support of the Bible if he had been able to answer Sonia wisely and gently, "It may be the same with Polenka. We must not count on God to prevent these tragedies, nor must we blame him if they happen. God is not our protector *against* trouble. He is our refuge and strength, a very present help *in* trouble."

This God is not dead but very much alive. He has shown himself to be alive in human experience, especially in the experience of the men who wrote the Psalms of the Old Testament. From the Psalmists we learn what God can be and what he can do in the experience of those who believe in him and trust him. The writer of the *46th Psalm* found him to be *a God who secures*—not against disaster but within disaster, not against the worst that can possibly happen but in spite of the worst that can possibly happen. The Psalm falls into three strophes or stanzas.

"God is our refuge and strength, a very present help in trouble. Therefore will not we fear, though the earth be removed, and though the mountains be carried into the midst of the sea; though the waters thereof roar and be troubled, though the mountains shake with the swelling thereof."

This is not science fiction—not any more. Indeed, there is something frighteningly modern about this paroxysm of nature —the earth convulsing, the mountains trembling, the ocean bed shuddering, and its waters roaring and churning. A few hydrogen bombs, strategically dropped, could produce exactly that effect; and in our world today it represents the very worst that could possibly happen. Overshadowing all our personal fears is the collective fear that local wars raging in remote corners of the globe will explode into a major war, engulfing the whole inhabited world in its fury. Now that we have invented the Frankenstein monster of ultimate annihilation we must live from day to day under the shadow of ultimate disaster.

Courageously the Psalmist faced up to a disaster of such magnitude. He reckoned with the possibility that the worst may happen to man's world and that God may allow it to happen. This is the only mature and realistic view of God's relationship to man's world. God has placed tremendous power in the hands of man, power which can do the world untold good but which, in a moment of folly or wickedness, could cause global catastrophe of the precise proportions graphically described in the

46th Psalm. To say innocently with poor Sonia that "God will not allow anything so awful" is to forget that God treats us not as puppets but as personalities. God entrusts power to man as a father entrusts the family car to his adolescent son. Having given him the ignition key, the father does not then control the vehicle by remote radio. He hopes and prays that the boy will drive responsibly, as he has been taught to do, but he knows, every time his son takes the car on the road, that the worst may happen and that he, the father, cannot prevent it happening.

The Psalmist comes to terms with this fact in the relationship between God and man. He faces up to the very worst that can happen. He does not say that it *will* happen—after all, no one can absolutely predict a flood or an earthquake or even a war—but he does reckon with these disasters as a possibility in man's life upon this earth. They may happen, and God may allow them to happen. Yet the amazing thing about the Psalmist is that, having dismissed, or not even taken into account, the idea of God as a Guardian Angel, he still finds in his relationship to God a sense of security. He does not say, "We will not fear *that* the earth be removed," but he does say, "We will not fear, *though* the earth be removed." The God of his experience is still a God who secures—not against disaster but within disaster, not against the worst that can happen but in spite of the worst that can happen.

The great Christians have all found this larger security in God. To Paul the Apostle there was one eternal, dependable and unchanging reality in the world of our experience— *the love of God;* not his own conviction of God's love but the historical demonstration of God's love in the life, death and resurrection of Jesus Christ. Paul's conviction was that nothing could ever come between him and that love. As though to prove his point Paul in his Roman Letter conjures up all the enemies of personality, all the terrors that destroy faith and assurance, and he dares them to do their worst. Tribulation, distress, persecution, famine, nakedness, peril, sword—all had left their marks on Paul's body but none had broken through to his soul, none destroyed his inner sense of well-being, his sense of security in God. Like the Psalmist, Paul had a realistic view of God's relationship to the world. He saw the love of God not as a wall that stands between us and disaster but rather as the stronghold of our souls and the source of our courage in the midst of disaster. That was why he could declare in the spirit of the Psalmist, "For I am persuaded, that neither death, nor life, nor angels, nor principalities, nor powers, nor things present, nor things to come, nor height, nor depth, nor any other creature be able to separate us from the love of God, which is in Christ Jesus our Lord."

"There is a river, the streams whereof shall make glad the city of God, the holy place of the tabernacles of the most High. God is in the midst of her; she shall not be moved: God shall help her, and that right early. The heathen raged, the kingdoms were moved: he uttered his voice, the earth melted. The Lord of hosts is with us; the God of Jacob is our refuge."

When the barbarian hordes were attacking Rome, a Bishop, nearly sixty years of age, sat down in that hour of darkness and despair to write a book which has since become one of the great classics of Christian literature. Augustine called his book, *Concerning the City of God,* and this, in effect, is what he said to his readers: "You thought that the passing of Rome and of the stability which she gave to the world meant the end of everything from the point of view of the Church. You were utterly wrong. Rome was an earthly city and shall not be everlasting. The Church is Divine and therefore indestructible. Human cities may rise and fall, but the City of God remains . . ."

In that sense, perhaps, we may interpret the Psalmist's words when he writes of "the city of God" which "shall not be moved", because "God is in the midst of her" and "God shall help her, and that right early." We cannot give them literal meaning, because they do not correspond with any facts. There is no safe and secure place in the midst of natural and social cataclysm, no miraculous city of man that will stand untouched and unpolluted by the destructive fury of an atomic war. There is only the City of God, the continuing community of God's love, the sanctuary of God's presence in the souls of men. This alone will survive as it has survived the raging of nations bent on conquest, whole populations in captivity, kingdoms tottering beneath the sword of revolution and tyranny. If the whole earth does melt in the crucible of a hydrogen blast, only the City of God will emerge purified. Only in that City can we seek refuge and find peace. Only in that City can we be secure.

Such is the faith of the 46th Psalm which inspired Martin
Luther to compose his great battle-hymn of the Reformation,

> "And though they take our life,
> Goods, honour, children, wife,
> Yet is their profit small;
> These things shall vanish all:
> The city of God remaineth".

Perhaps we can go a step further and infer from the 46th
Psalm that there are certain spiritual values that will survive
even the worst catastrophe. These values are invulnerable because they have their origin in God and because they are the
values that became flesh in Jesus. There was *truth* in Jesus—
no falsehood, no double-talk, but frankness, candour, integrity,
the transparent honesty of a man towards his fellow-men. There
was *goodness* in Jesus. When people looked at him they knew
that here was a character as clean as the driven snow; here was
human nature as God created it and life as God intended it to
be lived. There was *love* in Jesus—eyes that beheld in every
creature a brother man, lips that spoke only words of kindness
and compassion, hands that reached out in service to the
lowliest need. After the crucifixion scene in John Masefield's
Good Friday one character says to another, "Friend, it is now,
the tears, the cries, the pains; only the truth remains . . ."
Truth does remain because it is stronger than falsehood; goodness remains because it is greater than evil; love remains because it outlives hatred. Men can nail these values to a cross,
as they did once nail them to a Cross, but they cannot destroy
them, because they are rooted and grounded in the eternal
God.

We find security by consciously relating our lives to these
eternal values. Here is what it means in terms of personal
experience:

> "We were to learn that man has no rights in his imagined
> security. In how few moments can its bulwarks be under-
> mined! It seemed as if a tottering spire came crashing through
> our shuddering roof, walls meeting as they collapsed into
> the wreckage; everything smudged, smeared, senseless, silly
> chaos. 'I have to tell you,' the specialist said to me alone,
> when the diagnosis was clear, 'That we have no cures.' He

knew we wanted the whole truth . . . I left the hospital dazed."

These words tell their own story. You can read them in a book called *Triumph Over Fear*,[1] written by D. M. Wilson, a middle-aged man whose wife's sudden illness was diagnosed as progressive muscular atrophy. Two years later, after a heroic struggle, she died. It is the kind of disaster that could hit any one of us and it shows with stark realism that in this world there are no earthly securities, no material things, no human relationships, that cannot be snatched away from us. But that is not the end of the story, because this man and his wife were religious people; and the disaster, instead of shattering their faith in God, brought them to a deeper dependence upon God. Deprived of an endless future, they learned to accept and use each day as a gift from God. Restricted in body, they found joy in the deeper values of the soul. Beyond human help, they prayed without ceasing, not for what they wanted but for God's will to be done. They placed their hands in the hand of God and together walked through the darkness with courage, serenity, cheerfulness and love; and in the end even their facing of death was a triumph of the spirit.

"Come, behold the works of the Lord, what desolations he hath made in the earth. He maketh wars to cease unto the end of the earth; he breaketh the bow, and cutteth the spear in sunder; he burneth the chariot in the fire. Be still, and know that I am God: I will be exalted among the heathen, I will be exalted in the earth. The Lord of hosts is with us; the God of Jacob is our refuge."

But that seems to contradict all that has gone before. Having faced up to the worst that can possibly happen, having declared that he will be secure in the city of God no matter what happens, the Psalmist now seems to revert to the naïve faith of young Sonia who said, "God would not allow anything so awful." It is the mood that looks at the uncertain future with apparent realism and faces the dreadful possibility of man's misuse of his own freedom, then comforts itself by saying, "God would not allow anything so awful as a nuclear war. Despite man's

[1] Victor Gollancz Ltd., London, 1966.

stupidity, God will step in and prevent it. God can do that because he is God and he can do anything."

It reduces the practice of religion to the level of a boat drill. A few hours after an ocean liner puts to sea there is a warning blast from the ship's horn, and the passengers are summoned to put on their life jackets and report to muster stations. The captain and crew treat this exercise seriously. They inspect the life jackets and they lower the lifeboats, they pay attention to the smallest details because they know that the smallest detail can mean the difference between life and death in the event of a real disaster. The passengers usually treat the whole show as a bit of a lark. They laugh and joke and generally become acquainted with one another, then hurry off to the bar for a quick drink before lunch. They do so because they do not expect that God will not allow it to happen. God will protect the ship against storm, he will extinguish a fire, he will hold off enemy bombs, he will stop an epidemic of sickness from spreading. If that is not what the Psalmist means in the closing strophe, what does he mean?

I think he means nothing more and nothing less than that God's purpose will never be defeated. It is his way of asserting the great truth of God's sovereign control. There may be a storm, and the ship may be wrecked, and lives may be lost, but God is still master of the crisis. He can still bring blessing out of tragedy and make all things work together for good. It is not easy to grasp and understand this truth. I began to outline this chapter at a time when a huge mountain of coal slag, loosened by torrential rains, descended upon the Welsh village of Aberfan and buried little children alive. Try telling their grief-stricken parents that there is a God in heaven, a God who, though he could not prevent this senseless, man-made tragedy, can still redeem it, still weave it into the fabric of his sovereign purpose. Yet this is what the Psalmist would have us believe about God, and he is so convinced of its truth, so certain of God's sovereign control, even over the worst chaos, that he dare not say it himself but puts the words into God's own mouth, *"Be still, and know that I am God."*

Let us be very clear what we mean when we use the name "God". The Ground and Depth of all being; the uncreated Source of all creation; He who was before all things and who will be when they are gone; He who made all things and in whom all things consist; He who is perfect in wisdom and holiness, in righteousness, justice and love; He whose will is sovereign, who holds his hand on all passing events and directs them according to his purpose; He, the all-sufficient, all-powerful One, than whom there is nothing mightier in the universe—if that is what we mean by "God", we had better understand that in this world there are some forces, however awesome, however terrifying, that are not God. The space rocket is not God, nor the hydrogen bomb, nor the ocean storm, nor the landslide, nor cancer, nor insanity, nor violent death, because these things are not sovereign; they shall not have the last word in life and the world. But how can we describe God? How can finite language encompass the infinite? Even to try would be to describe not God but something less than God. We cannot really talk *about* God at all. We can only talk *to* him and listen to him and, as the Psalmist says, be still and behold his mighty works in history.

"*Come, behold the works of the Lord, what desolations he hath made in the earth* . . ." Yes, we shall behold the desolation of Calvary, God's mightiest work, the supreme event in all history through which God has once and for all declared his mastery over the worst that can possibly happen. We look at the Cross, empty, deserted, nothing but a spectre against the blackening sky, and we see it as the failure of man's worst to annihilate God's highest and best. We look at the Cross and remember that out of its defeat God brought victory, out of its weakness he brought strength, out of its suffering he brought comfort, out of its death he brought life. We look at the Cross and we know that the God with whom we have to do is alive and active and sovereign. This God will be exalted among the heathen. He will be exalted in the earth. He is the God who secures. "The Lord of hosts is with us; the God of Jacob is our refuge."

F

GOD PARDONS

A personal friend, for whom I have high regard, never grows tired of saying that the Church has an unhealthy obsession with sin. He suggests that, if a modern pagan wandered into a church on Sunday morning and listened to the morbid confessions of guilt in our hymns, prayers and sermons, he would think that he had wandered by mistake into a prison or into the psychiatric ward of a hospital. My friend blames the Apostle Paul who, he suspects, was something of a psychopath. Paul never forgave himself for persecuting the early Christians and he projected his guilt into his theology which has unfortunately eclipsed the simple teachings of Jesus in its influence on Christian thought and has created within the Church an unhealthy obsession with sin.

Let it be admitted that the Church is indeed the one organization in the world whose members meet together regularly to describe themselves as "miserable sinners". But why hold Paul exclusively responsible? His New Testament letters comprise only a fraction of Holy Scripture, and even if we expurgate them we still have the rest of the Bible which is no less emphatic than Paul in dealing with the "unhealthy" subject of sin. The very opening chapters, which tell in pictorial language the beginnings of man's life upon this earth, make it clear that one of the first facts to enter man's world was that disobedience against God which we call "sin". The great prophets of Israel, in their passionate crusade for social justice, fearlessly declared that the great fact which polluted the social organism was the fact of man's sin. Most of the so-called "simple teachings of Jesus" were addressed to sinners. One has only to follow his ministry in the Gospels in order to see that he deliberately sought out sinful people and made them face up to the fact of their sin.

So, if the Church seems to be obsessed with sin, it is only because the Bible as a whole is obsessed with sin. How can it be otherwise? The Bible is a record of human experience, and sin is a cardinal fact of human experience. Should you doubt this fact, read the newspaper headlines which are mainly the announcement of crime, sex, dishonesty, violence, corruption and war. Should you still doubt the reality of sin, take a walk down "Skid Row" in any city and look at the pimps, prostitutes, junkies, dope-pushers and meths-drinkers; or simply meet one of your more depressed and irritable friends in a moment of moral honesty and ask him what's troubling him. We live in a moral world, and whether our standards take their authority from God or from man, we know when we have violated them and we don't feel right about it. In fact, a man with any moral sense at all will be more troubled about his misdeeds and failures than about anything else in his life.

Such a man was the author of the *51st Psalm*. Tradition identifies him as King David and associates this outburst of penitence with the aftermath of a disgraceful episode in his career. David was a man with the ladies and, when he wanted a woman, he took her, even though she rightfully belonged to somebody else. At the height of his power he became infatuated with the beautiful Bathsheba, wife of one of his military officers, and made her pregnant. David solved that problem by arranging to have her husband lead a suicide squad into battle where he was killed. Then, conveniently forgetting his intrigue, he gave the man a military funeral and promptly married his widow. Some historians date the break-up of David's kingdom from precisely that point. Nature itself protested against the heinous crime. The heavens withheld their moisture, and drought paralyzed the land, cutting off subsistence for man and beast. Something had obviously angered God, and David suspected that he knew what it was. With adultery and murder on his conscience, the Hebrew king had more-than-sufficient reason to be obsessed with his sin.

Even if we had not a clue as to the author's identity we could still be certain that the 51st Psalm was written by a man obsessed with his sin. The Psalm stands on its own feet as one of the most poignant confessions of guilt in all sacred literature, and there is little wonder that its words and phrases have been woven into the great prayers and liturgies of the Church. The author, whoever he was, must have had something on his conscience to make him cry out, "*For I acknowledge my transgressions: and my sin is ever before me.*" In the case of David we can well imagine that his sin *was* ever before him. We can imagine that he was reminded of it from morning till night every time he looked at Bathsheba and that, when he fell into restless sleep, he saw her dead husband's face in his dreams. How could the Psalmist help being obsessed with his sin? It was the biggest problem in his life.

By the time he wrote the Psalm he had reached a point where he knew himself incapable of dealing with the problem. This is another cardinal fact of human experience. When a man who is a moralist violates what he knows to be the moral law he cannot forgive himself precisely because he *is* a moralist. He knows that forgiveness has to come from beyond himself. This is often the point where a man turns to God. This is the point where he stops calling his wrong-doing by fancy psychological names and gives it its proper name before God—"*Against thee, thee only, have I sinned, and done this evil in thy sight.*" This is the point where he begins to pray.

What does the Psalmist pray for? Four things: First, his sin makes him feel dirty inside, and he prays that God will make him clean. "*Wash me throughly from mine iniquity, and cleanse me from my sin . . . Purge me with hyssop, and I shall be clean: wash me, and I shall be whiter than snow . . . Create in me a clean heart, O God; and renew a right spirit within me.*" Second, the sense of guilt weighs so heavily on his mind that his mind has passed part of the burden to his body and made him physically ill. Out of pain and despondency he cries to God, "*Make me to hear joy and gladness; that the bones which thou hast broken may rejoice.*" Third and worst of all, his sin has broken his friendship with God, and he knows that only God can repair it. "*Cast me not away from thy presence; and take not thy holy spirit from me. Restore unto me the joy of thy salvation; and uphold me with thy free spirit.*"

One word describes the great thing that his wretched man asks of God—the word "pardon". He knows that he is guilty and he knows that in his agony of body and mind, in the fracture of his friendship with God and with man, he is getting exactly what he deserves. He knows also that he cannot expiate his wrong-doing. Nothing *he* can possibly do can atone for the double crime which he has committed. Before God he stands condemned, and his only hope is in something that God may do, something utterly undeserved and supernatural. He prays for it: "*Have mercy upon me, O God, according to thy lovingkindness: according unto the multitude of thy tender mercies blot out my transgressions.*"

One of the thrilling scenes in English literature comes at the close of Nordhoff and Hall's great historical novel, *Mutiny on the Bounty.* Some seamen stand on trial before a British Navy court-martial, accused of having wilfully seized their ship on the high seas and cast their captain and ship-mates adrift in a small boat. They are found guilty and sentenced to be hanged. Roger Byam, a young midshipman, faces death along with the others. In the eyes of the law he also stands condemned; but influential friends, not because they believe him to be innocent but because they know him to be basically a person of loyalty and integrity, go to the Prime Minister and plead for mercy. Roger Byam is granted a free pardon by His Majesty the King. Though judged guilty, he is acquitted, restored to his rank, and the record of his crime blotted out as though it had never happened. A King's Pardon—that is what the guilty Psalmist dared to ask of God. He had no other hope.

Every man, who has any moral sense at all, comes sooner or later to a place where nothing can restore his integrity but the free pardon of God. He has done something so extraordinarily vile in his own eyes and in the eyes of decent people that he could not atone for it or make reparation even if he lived a thousand years. In the sight of God he stands condemned, yet he must stand in the sight of God because he has nowhere else to go, no place on earth where he can recover his self-respect and live again as a moral man in moral society. He wants to be forgiven, yet he cannot forgive himself, nor can he expect those whom he has hurt to forgive him. Only God can forgive him, the God whose laws he has broken and whose love he has betrayed. His one hope is that the King of Heaven will be merciful and will do for him what that other king did for the guilty Roger Byam—pardon him freely, restore him to his status as a man and blot out the record of his sin as though it had never been committed. To God he can offer no prayer except the prayer of the Hebrew Psalmist, "Have mercy upon me, O God, according to thy lovingkindness: according unto the multitude of thy tender mercies blot out my transgressions."

"Nonsense!" retorts the humanist. "A man must pay for his

mistakes! Besides, how can you expect this God of yours, without compromising his justice, to answer such an audacious prayer?" It is a fair question, and we had better ask it ourselves. I read of a woman who told a pastoral counsellor that she had committed adultery with several men. It did not worry her that she had sinned against God. She was more worried that her friends would find out and disapprove. "God will forgive me," she said confidently. Surely she was taking rather a lot for granted. What reason had she to suppose, what reason had the Old Testament Psalmist to suppose that the God of man's experience forgives sins? This is the theological question and it must come first. It were sheer impertinence, if not blasphemy, to pray that God would grant us a King's Pardon for our sins unless we could believe with reason that the God with whom we have to do is, in fact, *a God who pardons*.

Concerning the gracious promise of Christ to be present at his Holy Supper, Thomas à Kempis writes, "Unless thou, O Lord, didst say this, who would believe it to be true?" We can write the same concerning God's gracious promise of pardon. Answering our own question, the only reason we have to suppose that the God of man's experience is a God who pardons is a reason that exists in God himself. We have hope that God will pardon us, not because we deserve his pardon but because he has declared himself to be a pardoning God. We come to the King of Heaven, not as Roger Byam came to the King of England, pleading our own basic loyalty and integrity, but pleading God's eternal promise of mercy and lovingkindness spoken in Scripture and proved in the experience of those who trust him.

As Christians, however, we rest our hopes not on promises alone. We dare to believe that our God is a pardoning God, not because of what he has said but because of something that he has done. We believe that there is a place of pardon, a place where a man can come with the heaviest burden of guilt on his conscience, a place where he stands condemned before God and yet where the surpassing action of God will be to lift that burden of guilt and to blot out his transgressions. That place is not a crowded palace where a king sits on his throne; it is lonely hill where a man hangs dying on a Cross. Perhaps we shall never understand everything about the Cross but we do understand enough to believe that God was on Golgotha and that the Cross was at once God's decisive judgment on our sins and his ultimate way of dealing with our sins. We believe that the Cross is God's mighty act on the stage of history in which he once and for all dramatized his eternal promise, made through patriarchs, prophets and psalmists, that there is no sin so great that he cannot and will not pardon the man who commits it. It is because of the Cross that we know our God to be a God who pardons. Because of the Cross we can boldly pray with the Old Testament Psalmist, "Have mercy upon me, O God, according to thy lovingkindness: according unto the multitude of thy tender mercies blot out my transgressions."

Over against the truth that the God of man's experience is a God who pardons, the Psalmist sets another truth crucial to our understanding of Divine forgiveness. He suggests that God does not pardon unconditionally. The pardon, promised in Scripture and made visible on the Cross, is not of the nature of an amnesty which automatically sets all men free from their guilt simply because they live within the order of God's redeeming love. Forgiveness is an intensely personal transaction between two parties. Unless a man enters such a relationship with God, the sight of a Cross in a church will no more alleviate his sense of guilt than the sight of a hammer-and-sickle in a Communist meeting-hall. There are conditions to God's pardon, and the writer of the 51st Psalm specifies some of them.

He suggests that the major condition is self-honesty. To God he prays, "*Behold, thou desirest truth in the inward parts: and in the hidden part thou shalt make me to know wisdom.*" It is precisely their failure to fulfil this condition of "truth in the inward parts" that makes it impossible for many people to receive the pardoning grace of God. The average person has an amazing capacity for self-deception. In any situation he will face up to every truth except the truth about himself and will set the blame everywhere except the place where it belongs. Not many of us are prepared to accept the discipline of self-honesty. It involves a terrific strain. It can be such a forbidding experience, so utterly painful and devastating that we smash everything in sight before submitting to so terrible an indignity.

Yet it was exactly that terrible experience which the prophet Nathan forced upon King David. At this time of national calamity, when the adulterous king sat sulkily on his throne, hurling the blame in all directions, Nathan came to him and said, in effect, "We have a problem and we need your judgment on it." Always a vain king as well as a just king, David leaned forward eagerly. Subtly the prophet told him of a rich man, possessing many flocks, who wanted to put on a dinner party with roast lamb as the main course. Instead of slaughtering one of his own animals he went to the house of a poor tenant and seized the only animal that the man possessed, a little ewe lamb which had been raised as a household pet for the children. David's sense of justice exploded. "As the Lord liveth," he thundered, "the man that hath done this thing shall surely die." Pointing at the outraged king, Nathan cried, "Thou art the man." David got the point of the parable. For the first time he faced the truth of his awful deed and laid the blame for the national calamity squarely where it belonged—on himself. As he stumbled into the sanctuary of God, the floodwaters of guilt burst through his dammed-up conscience and poured forth in this poignant confession of sin.

We can say again that, even if we had no clue as to its authorship, we could still recognize the 51st Psalm as a profound expression of self-honesty. Whatever he did to deserve God's punishment, the Psalmist calls his dread deed by no fancy names, nor does he plead the mitigating circumstances by which men usually seek to excuse their wrongs. To God he prays, "*Against thee, thee only, have I sinned, and done this evil in thy sight: that thou mightest be justified when thou speakest, and be clear when thou judgest.*" He frankly admits that he sinned, not because he made a mistake but because he is a sinner by nature: "*Behold, I was shapen in iniquity; and in sin did my mother conceive me.*" To make this confession of culpability before God was probably the most difficult, most humiliating thing he ever did but it was the condition of God's pardon, and the situation has not changed. When a man bears a burden of guilt on his conscience and he knows that he has no hope except in a free pardon from God, he knows also that God will not be impressed by religious piety but only by humble and abject self-honesty. So prays the Psalmist: "*For thou desirest not sacrifice; else would I give it: thou delightest not in burnt offering. The sacrifices of God are a broken spirit: a broken and a contrite heart, O God, thou wilt not despise.*"

Among the hymns which many moderns consider vulgar both musically and theologically are some of the hymns of John Newton.

> "Amazing grace! how sweet the sound,
> That saved a wretch like me!
> I once was lost, but now am found,
> Was blind, but now I see."

Poor poetry, to be sure, but precious poetry because it reflects the personal experience of the poet. Newton had been a tough sea captain in the Royal Navy who prided himself on being an atheist and who ridiculed everything that was decent and religious. Put in command of a slave trader transporting human cargo from Africa, he sank to the depths of degradation and despair. On a voyage to England his ship was caught in a terrific storm. Somehow he knew that, if the ship was to be saved and that if he was to be saved, God would have to save them both. The storm subsided, and Newton returned home, a changed man. He never went to sea again. After great opposition and many difficulties he was ordained an Anglican priest, serving a parish in London where he exercised remarkable influence, especially upon William Wilberforce in his fight to abolish the slave trade. Newton never forgot the sins of his past life and he never ceased to pour out his heart's praise for the free pardon of God.

So it happens to the pardoned sinner, as the Psalmist predicted it would when he solemnly promised God, *"Then will I teach transgressors thy ways; and sinners shall be converted unto thee. Deliver me from bloodguiltiness, O God, thou God of my salvation: and my tongue shall sing aloud of thy righteousness. O Lord, open thou my lips; and my mouth shall shew forth thy praise."* A broken spirit made whole again, a life of uplifting influence, a heart filled with praise of God, and an undying mood of holy joy—these ineffable blessings await the man who seeks and receives the free pardon of God.

GOD SUPPORTS

A procession of people passes through my mind. Leading the line is Bill whose right arm hangs withered at his side. He is followed by Marjorie who cannot get married because she is dominated by demanding parents. Along comes Frank whose grown son is too retarded to hold a job but not retarded enough to be brought under control. In the distance I can see Mary whose husband is an alcoholic, and Tom who hates his job and is up to his ears in debt.

These people have one thing in common—they all bear burdens that slow down their footsteps and make the journey of life exceedingly difficult. The burdens are not always visible, because many people don't like to advertise their troubles, but look into their faces and you will see the lines of anxiety, look at their shoulders and you will see signs of strain. In fact, look long enough at this never-ending procession and you will recognize some of your friends; you may even recognize yourself. It is a rare person who goes through the journey of life without having to carry some kind of physical handicap or emotional weakness or family responsibility or vocational difficulty that no other person can carry for him. The Apostle Paul wrote an obvious truth when he said, "Every man shall bear his own burden."

The *55th Psalm* is the spiritual case-history of a man who learned to bear his burdens. Ultimately he cast his burden upon the Lord because he discovered that the God of man's experience is *a God who supports,* but he did not make that discovery about God until he had tried other expedients. One commentator calls the 55th Psalm "a crescendo of distress". Certainly it begins on that note as the Psalmist cries out, "*My heart is sore pained within me . . . I mourn in my complaint, and make a noise.*" Tradition ascribes the agonized outburst to King David and dates it during the crisis caused by the rebellion of his son, Absalom. That seems probable when we consider the descriptive phrases and the general mood of the

Psalm in the light of the history of Absalom's rebellion recorded in the Old Testament book of *Second Samuel*. Psalm 55 could easily be the complaint of a king driven into hiding, threatened by his enemies, betrayed by his most trusted friends and forced to see his capital city the scene of violence, strife and plunder. Yet, for our purposes, it doesn't really matter who composed the 55th Psalm, because there is something timeless about its poignant utterances. Here we see a man weighed down by the burden of private and public misfortune and here we see the history of his reaction to it. He reacts in three distinct ways, three patterns of behaviour which are common to all men as they try to manage the burdens which life compels them to carry.

The first impulse of the Hebrew poet is to escape. "*Oh that I had wings like a dove! for then would I fly away, and be at rest.*" We know exactly how he felt. We all have the escapist impulse. When the journey becomes rough and the burden back-breaking, we begin to toy with the idea of dropping out of the procession and in our minds we explore the various avenues of escape. A person exclaims, "I have had it! I can't go a step further! I can't take it any more! I feel like quitting the whole thing!"

This is nothing to be ashamed of. If we want to preserve our strength of body and sanity of mind we must find healthy and legitimate ways of gratifying the escapist impulse from time to time. We must devise safety valves that relieve the pressure and we must acquire absorbing interests that divert our attention and energies from the main business of living. That's why a good holiday is not a luxury but an investment. Every man owes it to himself at least once in twelve months to get as far away as he can from his house and his job and from everything that reminds him of the burdens that he must carry. There was a middle-aged professional woman who had not taken a holiday for years because she was tied to her elderly mother, and the old lady refused to leave the house or be cared for by anyone but her daughter. The daughter's friends could see that she was breaking under the strain and they pleaded with her to put her mother in a nursing home and go away for a few weeks. They were not asking her to get rid of the burden but only to lay it aside for a short time so that she could catch her breath and straighten her aching shoulders and recover strength before taking it up again. They were simply suggesting a legitimate and loving means of escape.

The escapist impulse becomes a neurosis only when we make it an obsession and allow it to dominate our thoughts and involve us in a world of fantasy. "*Oh that I had wings like a dove! for then would I fly away, and be at rest. Lo, then would I wander far off, and remain in the wilderness.*" What did David mean by "the wilderness"? Was it a geographical area or was it a state of mind? Was it a physical desert or was it an emotional release? In his book, *The Healing of Persons*,[1] Dr. Paul Tournier, the Swiss psychiatrist, has a penetrating chapter on Flight, the means by which men seek to escape their burdens. There is the flight into dreams, in which a man escapes from harsh reality into delightful fantasy. There is the flight into the past, in which a man tries to escape from the awareness of his present problems by walking with his head turned backwards. There is the flight into the future, where nebulous plans become an escape from the imperfections of the present. There is the flight into disease, in which we actually make ourselves ill to escape some difficult duty or to become the centre of attention. There is the flight into passivity, when life becomes a terrified inaction. There is the flight into work, where a man finds in his work an escape from a bleak and bitter situation. Worst of all, there is the flight into religion, where the house of God can be like an island cut off from the world and where religion and life are divorced.

Whenever he gulped down some whisky, and it was often, George used to grimace and say, "I hate this stuff. It will probably kill me some day, but it's the only thing that makes life bearable." Well, life was a pretty rough deal for George. He lived in pain all the time and he drank to escape from his pain. Alcoholism is an extreme form of escape, destructive to the personality; so is the L.S.D. "trip" which admits the addict to a psychedelic fairyland in technicolour. These escapist tactics are degrees of suicide. All grow out of the recognition that essentially our burdens are not a part of the environment but a part of ourselves and that we cannot escape them except by some degree of self-annihilation. The final route of escape is total self-annihilation, the route taken successfully by a

[1] Collins, New York.

quarter-million people every year and attempted unsuccessfully by three times that number. Of all the reasons that people leave behind them after they have resigned from the human race the commonest is this, "I wanted to get away from it all."

But most of us do not want to get away from it all; we do not want to annihilate ourselves. We want to go on living, not in some after-life but in this life, in spite of the burdens which it compels us to carry, because this life with all its back-breaking problems and responsibilities is the only life we know. Therefore we shall not throw down our burdens and cut loose from the procession and run away into some "wilderness" of physical, mental, moral or religious isolation. David toyed with that idea but he turned from it quickly, because its sheer unrealism only compounded his misery. The burdens are there, they have our names written on them; and we cannot get out from beneath them. We must learn to manage them some other way.

Since dove's wings cannot lift the weight off the human spirit, the Psalmist turns to another and more realistic expedient. "*Destroy, O Lord, and divide their tongues . . . Let death seize upon them, and let them go down quick into hell . . .*" It is a crude and almost inhuman prayer, this bloodthirsty petition that God will demoralize, destroy and permanently damn his enemies, but it marks an advance in the Psalmist's spiritual history. Prayer of any kind is a spiritual advance, because it means that we have consciously brought God into our experience; we have taken the first step towards God, humbly acknowledging that there are some things which we cannot do for ourselves but which God may be able and willing to do for us. Bloodthirsty or not, it was an instinctive prayer. The Psalmist did what we all do when life's burdens become unbearably heavy. He asked God to take away the burden, to remove it; and the instinct is not mistaken, because sometimes God does exactly that. There are burdens which, when we cannot manage them ourselves, we can actually give up to God. To pray about them is to hear God saying, "You need not carry these any more. You can leave them with me."

This is certainly true of some of the emotional burdens which weigh heavily upon our spirits and make our journey through life more difficult. Many people carry an unnecessary load of guilt. There is a parable in the incident of the American naturalist who found a dead eagle on the seashore with a large metal trap fastened to one of its feet. Hundreds of miles away on some mountain slope the huge bird had dropped into the jaws of this trap and, though by its great strength it had managed to lift the thing from the ground, yet fatally handicapped in its search for food, it had finally fallen at the margin of the sea to die of exhaustion.[1] In like manner many people carry around with them a crippling burden of guilt, a sense of shame over moral blunders committed years ago and now exaggerated out of all proportion in their minds. It saps their energy and depletes their resouces until, exhausted and defeated, they finally give up the struggle with the trap of torture still clinging to them. The tragedy of it is that they need not carry this burden of neurotic guilt. They can give it up to God. Let them once come to a Cross, the place of God's forgiving love, and like Bunyan's Pilgrim they will feel the burden loose from off their shoulders and fall from off their backs and begin to tumble and continue to do so until it comes to the mouth of a sepulchre where it falls in and they see it no more.

In answer to prayer God has lifted painful burdens from the bodies of men and women. Writing tenderly about his beloved wife, Clare, James Davidson Ross tells about the migraine headaches which she had suffered from the time of her youth. The attacks came every two or three weeks, of such intensity that she could not lift a finger for twenty-four hours; and the pain was so excruciating that it put her vision out of focus and distorted her speech. Doctors offered no hope of cure. The only thing to be done for her was to get her to bed as quickly as possible, darken the room and leave her alone to suffer. While Clare, in middle-age, was still feeling sick and wretched in the aftermath of one of her worst attacks, her husband took her to a chapel service at a place of Divine Healing where she prayed and received the laying on of hands. She left the chapel with all signs of migraine gone, and to the end of her life she never had another attack. Her husband writes, "The cynic may say that a psychosomatic complaint had been dealt with by psychological means: the cynic may say what he will . . . In

---

[1] Told by J. S. Bonnell in *No Escape from Life* (Harper and Brothers, New York, 1958), p. 66.

faith Clare had taken twenty years of sickness to God, and in faith she had left that sickness with him."[1]

What shall we say to the man of faith whose burden is not lifted, the person who prays passionately to God, yet remains crushed by its intolerable weight? Very gently we shall ask that person if he thinks that his prayers have brought him sufficiently close to God so that God can really do something for him. Because he wanted God to help him in a big way the writer of the 55th Psalm prayed in a big way: "*Evening, and morning, and at noon, will I pray, and cry aloud: and he shall hear my voice.*" Jesus taught that we should pray without ceasing and, to enforce his teaching, he told the story of an unjust judge who finally gave in to a poor woman's ceaseless importunity. The lesson is not that God needs to be coaxed and exasperated by our prayers but that, if by our persistence we can influence an impersonal earthly magistrate in our favour, how much more the Heavenly Father who knows us and cares what happens to to us. If you really want something that only God can give you, then prove how seriously you want it by saying your prayers three times a day. That God has not yet taken away your burden does not mean that he will not or cannot take it away. It could mean that the Father God, who cares for the total development of your personality, is withholding the miracle of his grace and power until you are spiritually prepared to receive it.

It could also mean that God's answer to your prayer is "No". So it had to be with the Psalmist, and he knew it. His was an unreasonable prayer, an affront to God's character as holy, righteous love. Naïvely he asked God to destroy his enemies, but God does not kill off bad people simply because they fight against good people, nor does he lift every burden simply because the man who carries it happens to be a man of faith. Consider it possible that some of our burdens ought not to be removed. They keep us balanced, they bring out our qualities of endurance, they make men of us, they hold us up by holding us down. Stanley Jones once said, "All my life I have carried a cross. Recently that cross was lifted. Now I find myself praying for another cross, because the cross has made me what I am

[1] James Davidson Ross, *Clare* (Hodder and Stoughton, London, 1965), pp. 53–4, 130–31.

today." Removing our burdens is not the only way that God
has of answering our prayers. For our own good or for the good
of others God may ask us to keep a particular burden and at
the same time provide us with the strength to bear it. This
insight marks the highest point in the Psalmist's spiritual history.
He trusts God to support him and he exhorts all men of faith
to do the same. "*Cast thy burden upon the Lord, and he shall
sustain thee: he shall never suffer the righteous to be moved.*"

" . . . *and he shall sustain thee*". The thought here is not that
God is an external factor who enters our situation like a
Celestial Porter to give us a hand with the heavy baggage
that we must carry on life's journey. God works inside our
situation. He does not simply add *his* strength; he increases *our*
strength. God sustains us, he supports and strengthens us, so
that, while we continue to carry our own burdens, they do not
weigh intolerably on our bodies and souls. Somewhere I read
of an unusual bridge that crosses a river in Europe. Halfway
across it is a little wayside chapel. The writer said that his hotel
room overlooked the bridge and that he used to sit there and
watch the peasants on their way to and from market. When they
came to the small chapel they left their heavy bundles outside
and went in to pray. He noticed that, when they came out
again, they picked up the same bundles as if they had actually
been made lighter during the season of prayer. It recalls Long-
fellow's familiar lines:

> "Oft have I seen at some cathedral door
> A labourer, pausing in the dust and heat,
> Lay down his burden, and with reverent feet
> Enter, and cross himself, and on the floor
> Kneel to repeat his paternoster o'er;
> Far off the noises of the world retreat;
> The loud vociferations of the street
> Become an indistinguishable roar.
> So, as I enter here from day to day,
> And leave my burden at this minster gate,
> Kneeling in prayer, and not ashamed to pray,
> The tumult of the time disconsolate
> To inarticulate murmurs dies away,
> While the eternal ages watch and wait."

In his own experience the writer of the 55th Psalm discovered that the God with whom we have to do is a God who supports. In his own life he tested and proved the promise of a Hebrew prophet who said, "They that wait upon the Lord shall renew their strength." It is a promise that *has* to be tested in order to be proved. The first time I really grasped its reality was an occasion when I was having lunch with a Canadian cabinet minister, a man of amazing vitality who was noted for his relaxed manner and for the prodigious volume of work that he could produce in a single day. He told me that he never allowed himself more than six hours of sleep a night and that, when he entered the government and took on the burdens of his office, he reduced his sleeping hours to four. I asked him, "How do you keep going? How do you manage to carry this heavy responsibility? How do you stand up under all the strain and criticism?" In answer he opened his pocket diary and showed me words written on the inside cover, words that he consulted several times a day: "They that wait upon the Lord shall renew their strength." Like the Psalmist he had brought God into his experience and discovered him to be a God who supports, a God who does not always remove or even lighten our burdens but who, if we wait upon him and trust him and rest in him, will make our strength equal to any burdens that life compels us to carry.

Marc Connolly's play, *The Green Pastures*, closes with the Crucifixion. The angels in heaven can hear the human scream that rises from the earth: "Look at that man carrying his cross up the hill! That's a terrible burden for one man to carry!" A terrible burden, to be sure; but because God in Christ *has* carried it, because he has shared our life and borne our infirmities, we shall trust his promise that, whatever burden we must carry through the journey of life, if we cast it upon the Lord, he will sustain us.

G

GOD SURPASSES

One scarcely expects the Dean of an English cathedral to have a bias against Church music, but such was the case with Dean Inge of St. Paul's Cathedral in London. In his published *Diary* he implies that the surest way to drive religion out of the great prayers, creeds and passages of Scripture is to set them to music and put them at the mercy of a choir. Perhaps we can sympathize with the "gloomy Dean", especially with regard to some of the Psalm-settings, ancient and modern. There is a lugubrious Russian setting to the 103rd Psalm which even the most limited choirs used to sing with depressing frequency. It drags along in a minor key like a funeral dirge over the death of God. That was how it seemed to me until I once heard it sung by an American Negro male choir. These men redeemed this piece of music for me, they brought it to life, they sang it not slowly and mournfully but with rapid joy and exultation as a great outburst of praise to the living God.

That is certainly the mood of the *103rd Psalm*, a mood set by its familiar opening verse:

> "*Bless the Lord, O my soul: and all that is within me, bless his holy name.*"

At once we recognize it as the inspiration of some of the great, beloved hymns of the Church. We think of the Scottish paraphrase, "O Thou my soul, bless God the Lord . . ." We think especially of the majestic hymn, made more majestic ever since Her Majesty the Queen chose it as the processional hymn at her own wedding:

> "Praise, my soul, the King of heaven;
> To his feet thy tribute bring:
> Ransom'd, heal'd, restor'd, forgiven,
> Who like me His praise should sing?
> Praise Him, Praise Him, Praise Him, Praise Him,
> Praise the everlasting King."

Praise is not self-generating; it does not spring as a root out of dry ground. We feel no impulse to praise, no reason to give thanks for anything in this life as long as we are getting only what we deserve. Why thank your employer for your weekly pay envelope if you have earned its contents? Why should a child thank his parents for food, clothing, shelter and education? I heard of an adolescent who gave a mature answer to one of his teachers when she told him that he ought to be more grateful to his parents. He said, "I didn't ask to be born. My parents brought me into the world for their own enjoyment. They are only doing for me what I deserve. Why should I thank them?" In a sense we can take the same attitude to God. So God created us, but we didn't ask to be created. So God provides for us, but isn't that the natural obligation of a responsible father? Why give thanks to God when he is doing for us only what we deserve? Let God do for us more than we deserve, and we shall have reason to thank him.

Well then, read the 103rd Psalm, because that's what it is all about. A single theme runs through this mighty anthem of praise—the theme of God's grace. "Grace" is one of those religious words which has been worn thin with over-use like an old coin, so that now we hand it around freely, scarcely recognizing its true value. When a hospital patient confessed that she was having a hard time hanging on to her religious faith, I tried to comfort her by saying that in these days, when faith comes hard to all of us, the one certainty to which I still cling is my experience of the grace of God. "What is grace?" she asked; and for the moment I registered surprise that she, a Christian woman, should ask such a question. I tried to explain that grace means something extra in life, like the flowers and letters and get-well cards which she had received from kind friends, not because they were obligated to send them but because they wanted to send them; it was a gracious thing for them to do. The grace of God means God's extra, the way he deals with us beyond our deserving, the good things he gives us, not because he has to give them but because he wants to give them. That is what makes him God. In his goodness to men he goes further than we are willing to go, he does for us what no other person would ever do, he is *a God who surpasses* all our human limitations. He showed himself to be that kind of God in the experience of the Hebrew Psalmist; and if there

is a single admonition that can be inferred from the 103rd
Psalm, it is this: *Don't underestimate God!*"

The Psalmist says, *Don't underestimate the measure of
God's kindness*. There was a celebrated American preacher,
Dr. William Stidger, who used to write books filled with
human-interest stories of the important people whom he had
met. He tells that one Sunday, after visiting a mid-western
church as guest preacher, he was entertained for dinner at the
home of a retired missionary. He barely caught his host's name
which meant nothing to him. The old man kept talking about
his son, Henry. He told Dr. Stidger that Henry had tried a
number of journalistic ventures without success. Finally he and
a friend got the idea for a new kind of magazine but didn't
have the money to finance it, so he asked his father to lend
him the money. The retired missionary gave his son six hundred
dollars—his entire life's savings. Dr. Stidger says that he had
been forming an unfavourable image of Henry, when the old
man asked him, "You know my son, Henry, don't you?
Henry Luce?" Dr. Stidger suddenly realized who his host was—
the father and financial backer of Henry Luce, founder and
editor of *Time*, *Life* and *Fortune* magazines, one of the great
journalistic empires in the world.

Suppose the venture had failed? Only because it succeeded
so phenomenally do we refrain from thinking that here was a
young man who asked more than he had a right to ask of his
father. Surely his father had already done for him all that he
deserved. How could he have the colossal nerve to take the
old man's life's savings and gamble them on a chancy enterprise? We know the answer. We know that *not* to have sought
his father's help would have been seriously to underestimate
his father, because standing behind his own son to the very
limit of his resources is exactly what a kind father wants to do.
God, declares the Old Testament Psalmist, is kinder than the
kindest of human fathers. Imagine the utmost limits of parental
love, and God's goodness goes even beyond them.

> *"Bless the Lord, O my soul, and forget not all his benefits:*
> *Who forgiveth all thine iniquities; who healeth all thy diseases;*
> *Who redeemeth thy life from destruction; who crowneth thee*
> *with lovingkindess and tender mercies; Who satisfieth thy*

mouth with good things; so that thy youth is renewed like the eagle's . . ."

This is the God in whom Jesus taught men to believe, the gracious God whose kindness surpasses all our human limitations. To such a God we can confidently pray. Jesus prayed, with such an obvious sense of reality and power that his disciples begged him, "Lord, teach us to pray"; so he taught them and taught the whole human race the most perfect of all prayers which begins, "Our Father which art in heaven . . ." Jesus then told his disciples that they must never count any request too small or too great to bring before the Father God: "Ask, and it shall be given you; seek, and ye shall find; knock, and it shall be opened unto you." He was saying, in effect, "Don't be afraid to pray, don't grumble about your unworthiness, don't be pious and go about saying that God has already done for you all that you deserve and that you have no further claim on him. Your worthiness has nothing to do with it. God deals with you beyond your deserving. He gives, not because you have a claim on him but because he loves you and delights to give. That's what makes him God."

Jesus often said that we should know a great deal more about God if we did not try to cut him down to our size. We assume, for example, that because we cannot imagine God rearranging his own laws in order to answer our prayers, therefore God cannot rearrange his laws in order to answer our prayers. We assume that, because we find some people odious, therefore God must find them odious. "But it isn't that way at all," Jesus suggested. "God is not restricted to our human likes and dislikes. He doesn't divide people into his friends and enemies, showing kindness to one and not to the other. To suppose that he is that kind of God is to underestimate him." "Do you want to be like God?" Jesus asked, in effect, and he gave this actual reply: "Love your enemies, and do good, and lend, expecting nothing in return; and your reward will be great, and you will be sons of the Most High; for he is kind to the ungrateful and the selfish."

Kind to the ungrateful and the selfish—that's what makes him God and that is what makes him different from us. He is a gracious God. He surpasses the measure of human kindness. I found this truth summed up in a paragraph from an article written by a lawyer who does social work in New York's Harlem and who describes a young drug addict whom he has tried to help professionally and personally without much success:

"He is dirty, ignorant, arrogant, dishonest, unemployable, broken, unreliable, ugly, rejected, alone. And he knows it. He knows at last that he has nothing to commend himself to another human being. He has nothing to offer. There is nothing about him which permits the love of another person for him. He is unlovable. But it is exactly in his own confession that he does not deserve the love of another that he represents all the rest of us. For none of us is different from him in this regard. We are *all* unlovable. But more than that, the action of this boy's life points beyond itself to the gospel: to God who loves us though we hate him, who loves us though we do not satisfy his love, who loves us though we do not please him, who loves us not for our sake but for his own sake, who loves us freely, who accepts us though we have nothing acceptable to offer him. Hidden in the obnoxious existence of this boy is the scandalous secret of the Word of God."[1]

Next, the Psalmist says, *Don't underestimate the scale of God's forgiveness.* One of the most natural questions in the Bible is the one that Peter asked Jesus, "Lord, how often shall my brother sin against me, and I forgive him? As many as seven times?" That sounds generous enough even by our standards. Most of us would consider ourselves very long-suffering if we allowed someone, even someone we love, to hurt us seven times and each time said to him, when he came crawling back, "I forgive you." Surely there is a point beyond which forgiveness cannot be reasonably expected to go. A survivor of one of the most brutal Nazi concentration camps, a boy who had to watch his relatives killed before his very eyes, writes a devastating book entitled *I Cannot Forgive*; and who can blame him for it? A man would have to be more than human to forgive the most monstrous crime in history.

It *was* a more-than-human Man who prayed on a Cross for his murderers, "Father, forgive them; for they know not what they do." Only God forgives and goes on forgiving even when

[1] *The Christian Century*, May 10, 1961.

men reject him and torture him and nail him to a tree and leave him there to die. That is what makes him God. His forgiveness surpasses all our human limitations. Such was the God of whom the Psalmist sang out of a full heart:

> "*The Lord is merciful and gracious, slow to anger, and plenteous in mercy. He will not always chide: neither will he keep his anger for ever. He hath not dealt with us after our sins; nor rewarded us according to our iniquities. For as the heaven is high above the earth, so great is his mercy toward them that fear him. As far as the east is from the west, so far hath he removed our transgressions from us. Like as a father pitieth his children, so the Lord pitieth them that fear him. For he knoweth our frame; he remembereth that we are dust.*"

In his satire, *The Great Divorce*, C. S. Lewis takes us with a busload of ghosts who have made an excursion from hell to heaven with a view to remaining there permanently. They meet the citizens of heaven, the "solid people". One very Big Ghost is astonished to find in heaven a man who on earth was tried and executed for murder. "What I'd like to understand," he explodes, "is what you're here for, as pleased as Punch, you, a murderer, while I've been walking the streets down there and living in a place like a pigsty all these years". The solid person tries to explain that he has been forgiven, that both he and the man he murdered have been reconciled at the judgment seat of God, but the Big Ghost isn't having any of it. The injustice of the situation staggers him. "My rights!" he keeps shouting. "I've got to have my rights same as you, see!" "Oh, no," the solid person assures him. "It's not as bad as that. I haven't got my rights, or I should not be here. You will not get yours either. You will get something far better."[1]

That is what staggered the Apostle Paul—the fact that he did not get his "rights" from God; he got something far better. What were the "rights" of a man who had been the chief of a religious Gestapo, breaking into the homes of his victims, dragging them out to be beaten and stoned and even killed? Some people accuse Paul of being obsessed with the fact of sin. It would be more true to say that he was obsessed with the fact that God had pardoned his sin. Paul never ceased to marvel at the surpassing scale of God's forgiving grace.

[1] Geoffrey Bles, London, 1962, pp. 30–4.

Instead of dealing with him as he deserved, God chose this former enemy of Christ to receive the highest favour that Christ could bestow. God made him a witness of the Resurrection. Writing to the Corinthians about the appearances of the Risen Christ to his apostles, Paul adds in sheer wonder, "Last of all, as to one untimely born, he appeared also to me. For I am the least of the apostles, unfit to be called an apostle, because I persecuted the church of God. But by the grace of God I am what I am . . ." Paul was really saying to his readers, "If God can forgive me, he can forgive anyone".

There are people who doubt that truth. Many a man, looking back over a life of dissipation, dishonesty and selfishness, will simply dismiss any overtures of religion by saying harshly or wistfully, "Don't talk to me of God's forgiveness. God could never forgive anyone as bad as I have been." If you are that man you need to be told that you seriously underestimate God. You restrict him by your own human standards. You forget that what makes him God is the fact that he surpasses our human standards. He forgives and goes on forgiving beyond the capacity of our minds to imagine. Should you doubt that fact, push your way through the maze of things to a Cross and listen to that dying Man praying "Father forgive them," not only for his first century crucifiers but for all who crucify him afresh by their stubborn refusal to accept his will for their lives. One truth hangs like a caption in the sky above the dark picture of Calvary, a truth which avails for you: "Where sin abounded, grace did much more abound."

The 103rd Psalm says to us also, *Don't underestimate the extent of God's mercy*. Thornton Wilder wrote an unusual play called *The Skin of our Teeth*[1] which has to be seen in order to be appreciated. It casts a typical American family, named Antrobus, in the role of the human race and it spans the whole of recorded history. Each act brings mankind to the brink of ultimate disaster, first with the approaching ice age, then with the flood, finally with the Second World War. Each time the human race appears doomed, but each time some unexpected factor miraculously intervenes; and man, despite his own stupidity, is saved by the skin of his teeth. Mr. Antrobus himself sums up the story in one of his closing speeches: "Oh

[1] Samuel French Ltd., Toronto.

I've never forgotten for a long time that living is a struggle. I know that every good and excellent thing in the world stands, moment by moment, on the razor edge of danger and must be fought for . . . All I ask is the chance to build new worlds, and God has always given us that second chance, and has given us voices to guide us, and the memory of our mistakes to warn us . . ."

That is what the Bible means by the mercy of God. That is what the Psalmist means when he writes,

"As for man, his days are as grass: as a flower of the field, so he flourisheth. For the wind passeth over it, and it is gone; and the place thereof shall know it no more. But the mercy of the Lord is from everlasting to everlasting upon them that fear him, and his righteousness unto children's children; To such as keep his covenant, and to those that remember his commandments to do them."

The Psalmist is saying that the one constant factor that runs like a thread through history and holds history together is the unmerited grace of God. You and I, if we sat on the throne of the universe and tried to govern the world for five thousand years, or even for five years, would give up in disgust; but God's patience surpasses ours, and to project our own limitations upon God is seriously to underestimate the extent of his mercy.

Here the Psalmist is writing not as an individual but as a member of a nation, a spiritual community. Commentators date the 103rd Psalm in the years after the Jews were released from exile in Babylon and allowed to return to their homeland—which would indeed be a time when children gave thanks to God that he had faithfully kept the covenant made with their fathers. The whole story of the Old Testament is the story of a faithful God keeping covenant with his people and, even when they break the covenant, stubbornly refusing to let it be broken but reaching beyond the sins of the fathers to visit his mercy upon the children. It is the story of the Church, the reason why we do not succumb to the popular pessimism about the Church's future but cling instead to the hope that God's surpassing mercy will extend even beyond the Church's present weakness and seeming irrelevance. It is the reason why we do not despair over the titanism of our technological age but cling instead to the hope that God's surpassing mercy will extend even beyond the blundering efforts of proud man to defy him.

Have we grounds for such hope? Let us look again at *The Green Pastures*, the story of God and his people as seen through the eyes of an old Negro preacher. The Play tells us that God has created a good earth and has made man to love and serve him, but proud man rebels against God and chooses to live life on his own terms, turning his earthly paradise into a hell. At last God seems to lose patience and appears ready to let man destroy himself, when suddenly he learns of an obscure prophet, Hosea, whose wife has been unfaithful to him, yet who still loves her and clings to her and will not let her go. In a moment God knows that this is how he must deal with men— not by abandoning them to self-destruction but by meeting them where they are and suffering with them and for them. In its closing scene the play brings us to a Cross—God's final demonstration in history that he deals with us not as we deserve but with inexhaustible mercy. That is what makes him God. Never underestimate the kindness, the forgiveness, the mercy of this gracious God who gave his Son to die upon a Cross. Praise him with all Creation, praise him with all the saints, praise him with all your heart and soul. So sings the writer of the 103rd Psalm:

> "*The Lord hath prepared his throne in the heavens; and his kingdom ruleth over all. Bless the Lord, ye his angels, that excel in strength, that do his commandments, hearkening unto the voice of his word. Bless ye the Lord, all ye his hosts; ye ministers of his, that do his pleasure. Bless the Lord, all his works in all places of his dominion: bless the Lord, O my soul.*"

GOD RESCUES

I enjoy going through an art gallery but, because I am basically an unsophisticated person, I prefer the paintings I can understand. That is what appeals to me about the *107th Psalm*. It is like a little art gallery. It consists of four word-pictures that tell their own story, pictures which even a child can understand. First, a caravan lost in the desert, the camels standing idly while the exhausted travellers, faint with hunger and thirst, gaze frantically over the endless miles of sun-soaked sand. Second, a picture of prisoners in a dark dungeon, brought to this death-house by their own crimes, their ankles chained to the wall, their haggard faces emptied of all hope. Third, a place of sickness where the patients sit like skeletons, incapable of doing anything for themselves, refusing to eat and over-shadowed by the stinking miasma of death. Fourth, the picture of a storm at sea, monstrous waves buffeting a helpless ship, and the sailors staggering crazily about its deck as if they were drunk.

When we study these four pictures we see that they have one thing in common: they all portray a condition of helplessness. Skilfully this artist-with-words has visualized our human predicaments in symbolic terms that we can easily understand. The desert travellers represent many people today who are lost in a wilderness of existence and cannot find the way to the city of their souls. Some are lost in a desert of loneliness, vainly searching for human love and friendship but surrounded by people as numerous and impersonal as the sand. Some are lost in a wasteland of futility, a dreary circle of monotonous routine, with no sense of direction and purpose. Some are lost in a desert of affluence, rich in things but poor in soul, hungering and thirsting for the bread and water of life. Some feel lost in an uncaring universe, longing to find a source of security and stability but driven by forces as cruel and irresistible as the desert wind.

Other people are like those prisoners, trapped in the dungeon of their own moral folly, the victims of evil rather than the doers of it. They started out with freedom of choice but they continued to choose the wrong thing until finally it mastered them and they had no choice left. The drug addict would give anything to be set free from the chains of his "spike and syringe", but his habit has him "hooked", and he knows that the end of it will be death. In sober moments the alcoholic hates himself for the hell that he creates in his own home, but his bottle is like a chain, and he knows that he cannot break loose from it. So with the sex pervert and the compulsive gambler. No use telling these people to reform. They cannot reform; they are imprisoned in the dungeon of their own helplessness.

There have always been people like the third group who became emotionally and physically ill under the nagging of a tormented conscience. When the Psalmist describes the symptoms of neurotic guilt—failing strength, loss of appetite, approaching death—he could be describing Martin Luther as a young monk in the monastery at Erfurt. "Oh, my sin! My sin!" he moaned as he lay helpless on the cot in his cell. We might call him a psychopath until we read the medical case-books which tell of many disorders of the mind and body that people suffer only as a result of their own foolishness. Medical science cannot cure them. It may treat their symptoms but it says finally, as the doctor said of Lady Macbeth, "This disease is beyond my practice . . . More needs she the divine than the physician."

The panic of the storm-tossed sailors is a true picture of our human predicaments. Any man who has been to sea knows that life may be compared to an ocean voyage. There are calm, sunny days when the ship glides smoothly along, and all of life seems like a pleasure cruise. More often the ship has to plough through waves, the normal waves of sickness and sorrow and anxiety and disappointment, but the vessel has stabilizers and by careful handling it keeps on an even keel. Sometimes, however, with no warning, the ship can run into a violent storm when the gales of personal disaster and social calamity toss it crazily about and threaten to send it to the bottom of the sea. Then we feel helpless, we panic, we reel about the deck like drunken sailors, at our wit's end. So there is nothing fanciful about the little art gallery in the 107th Psalm. The four word-pictures are pictures of real life; they all portray conditions of human helplessness.

To please my children I took them to the cinema one afternoon and endured ninety minutes of harmless inanity. The film featured four phenomenally popular young men who played drums and electric guitars and kept crying out in tearful harmony, "Help me! Help me if you can?" That plaintive theme-song, which seemed utterly inane at the time, did not seem quite so inane the next time I heard it. Some clever television producers made it the theme music for a documentary film which showed the organized activity of patients in a mental hospital. One saw the pathetic sight of grown-up men and women unable to care for themselves, behaving like little children, having to be scolded or praised like the pupils in a kindergarten—all the time accompanied by this haunting background music, "Help me if you can!" as though it were the unuttered cry of their demented minds.

Those four groups in the 107th Psalm uttered that plaintive cry. Look closely at the travellers, the prisoners, the invalids and the sailors and you will see that they have another feature in common: their faces are turned upwards, and their lips form a single word, "Help!" In each case they knew that they had exhausted their human resources and that they had no hope of being released from their predicament unless some kind of help came from beyond themselves. In their helplessness they prayed, they brought God into their experience, they looked up and sent an "S.O.S." signal to heaven, "Help me! Help me if you can!" In each case the Psalmist uses the phrase, *"Then they cried unto the Lord in their trouble . . ."*

Someone will remind me that I am unsophisticated not only culturally but theologically as well. I shall be told, with or without charity, that the religion which takes man's helplessness as its starting-point is precisely the religion that modern man has rejected. This old-fashioned theology belongs to the days of man's childish dependence when there was so much that he did not know and so many things that he could not do for himself that he needed to think of God in terms of a Father-figure to whom he could pray for hlep. But all this has changed now. Man has come of age, he has learned to master his world and handle his predicaments, so why should he pray any more when there is really nothing left to pray for? A character in a modern novel speaks for man-come-of-age when he replies to a woman who tells him to ask Jesus for help, "I don't need no help from Jesus. I'm doing all right by myself."

It is a point of view which ought to be challenged, as, in fact, it is being challenged. In a recent book Bishop Lesslie Newbigin recalls conversing with a man who was a member of the team of physicists that worked on the first atomic bomb in Chicago during the final years of the Second World War. This man described the sudden change of feeling which came over him and his colleagues when they sensed their success and realized that the thing they had created was potentially the most monstrous evil ever set loose in the world. Because the nature of their work imposed absolute secrecy, they could not share their sense of anxiety and guilt with anyone outside; they had to work out the moral problem for themselves. The scientist told Bishop Newbigin how he and the others formed a series of groups to study every aspect of their problem—historical, ethical, religious, legal; how they bought and devoured books on subjects they had never studied before; how they finally wrote to President Truman urging that the bombs should be used only in some uninhabited area after due warning and not in any case on a city; how their letter was never even answered; and how they had to see the instrument they had created used to create the horrors of Hiroshima and Nagasaki. These scientists found that at the moment of their apparent triumph they were simply tools for an operation against which their moral sense revolted. Bishop Newbigin comments,

"A good deal is written at present about man's coming of age. Much of the traditional language of biblical religion is written off as belonging to a period when man felt himself unequal to the task of mastering his environment and when he had perforce to invoke the aid of alleged supernatural powers. Today, by contrast, it is suggested that man has grown out of this childish mentality. Today he knows how to control the powers of his environment . . . But this is only half the truth . . . Alongside of, or perhaps underneath, the sense of mastery, the assurance that we are only at the beginning of the development made possible by modern techniques, there is also a sense of something like meaninglessness and even terror as man faces his future . . ."[1]

Bishop Newbigin is saying that the picture of man in the 107th Psalm may not be so outdated as many moderns suppose. It may in fact, be an accurate picture of man today—trapped in a spiral of inexorable circumstance, doing what he does not want to do, making decisions that he does not want to make, swept by forces that he cannot control, man in a condition of helplessness crying out unconsciously to God, "Help me, if you can!"

We can put the truth in more personal terms. In the mid-1960s John Q. Citizen can live a fairly secure, useful and happy life without ever setting foot inside a church. Schools, universities, hospitals, labour unions, political parties and social agencies, within the growing framework of a welfare state, will meet most of his material and social needs. So why should he pray? Where does God fit into this vast scheme of man-made benevolence? What conceivable need can religion meet in his life? The obvious answer is—a need that touches the mainsprings of his personality. Concerning this modern pagan, John Q. Citizen, we could adapt Shylock's pathetic speech in *The Merchant of Venice:* "Hath he not eyes? Hath he not hands, organs, dimensions, senses, affections, passions? Fed with the same food, hurt with the same weapons, subject to the same diseases, healed by the same means, warmed and cooled by the same summer and winter as a Christian is? If you prick him, does he not bleed? If you tickle him, does he not laugh? If you poison him, does he not die?" At some point in his pre-packaged, cybernated existence John Q. Citizen, because he is still man and not God, will exhaust his human resources and will need help from beyond himself. At some point he will find himself among those four groups of whom the Psalmist wrote, "They cried unto the Lord in their trouble . . ."

We treasure the Old Testament Psalms, because they show us the many-sided activity of God in man's experience. They show him to be a living God who knows men personally and deals with them according to their needs and does for them

[1] Leslie Newbigin, *Honest Religion for Secular Man* (S.C.M. Press, London, 1966), pp. 30–1.

what they cannot do for themselves. The writer of the 107th Psalm, in a series of word-pictures, tells us that he found him to be *a God who rescues*. This is the next feature that the four groups have in common—though here the analogy of an art gallery ought to be changed, because the figures on the canvass begin to move, and the still-pictures become motion-pictures. In their helplessness the lost travellers, the prisoners, the invalids and the panic-stricken sailors cried to God for help, and in each case a factor from beyond themselves entered their situation and saved them. That saving factor was the activity of the living God. God pointed the desert travellers the way to a city, he broke the chains of the prisoners, he cured the sick, he stilled the storm. Each story closes with the phrase: *"Then they cried unto the Lord in their trouble, and he saved them out of their distresses."*

Though he draws them from real life the Psalmist wants us to know that the pictures in his little art gallery are intended to be symbolic. He wants us to know that what God did for these four groups he does for all men. To each picture he adds like a caption the same expression of longing: *"Oh that men would praise the Lord for his goodness, and for his wonderful works to the children of men!"* The Psalmist wants us to know that our God is at all times a God who rescues.

It is a theme that recurs constantly in the Psalms and makes them so precious in the experience of people who acknowledge their need of God. The distinguished actress, Helen Hayes, wrote a very moving article in which she told how the Psalms more than once brought her through a crisis, because she identified herself with the authors and made their prayers her own and found that God could be to her what he was to them. She tells of a time in her life when everything was going so well, and her cup so overflowed with happiness and success, that she lost all sense of God and drifted away from formal religion. Then came a moment of tragedy. Her daughter died, and Helen Hayes looked beyond herself for help. Desperately she reached out for God, but her hand struck only an emptiness; there seemed to be nothing or no one there. One night, as she tossed about sleeplessly in bed, she suddenly switched on the light and opened the Bible which she had not read for a long time. The Psalms came to her rescue, for as she read one of the great "Rescue Psalms" she found that she could talk to

God again, confident that he was listening to her and would help her as he had helped the Old Testament poet.[1]

Of course, we must resist the temptation to identify religion only with conditions of helplessness and the Church only with those predicaments that we cannot handle ourselves. There are too many people who do exactly that. Harry Emerson Fosdick published a memorable sermon entitled "Preventive Religion". Taking as his text the fine, familiar benediction from the *Epistle of Jude*, "Now unto him that is able to keep you from falling," he presents the proposition that religion is not simply a rescue party waiting at the foot of a precipice to pick up those who have fallen over; it is a fence at the top to prevent their falling over in the first place. We can develop the theme and say that religion exists not only to bring us through crises but to help us with the duties and relationships of routine living. Religion exists not only to redeem us from our moral failures but to give us through a lively faith in God the resources to live honourable and useful lives. Religion exists not only to help us overcome our weaknesses but to help us perfect our strength. Religion exists not only to comfort us in our affliction but to afflict us in our comfort.

This is all true, but it is also true that the God of man's experience is a God who rescues. He showed himself to be a rescuing God in the Psalmist's experience and in the experience of many of the men who wrote the Bible. He showed himself to be a rescuing God in Jesus Christ. Of all the titles by which believing Christians designate Jesus none is more precious and meaningful than the title "Saviour". His very name indicates it. Before his wondrous birth the angel said to his human father, ". . . you shall call his name Jesus, for he will save his people from their sins". His whole earthly ministry was a rescue operation to the very people described in the 107th Psalm. Jesus came to them in their helplessness, seeking and saving the lost, setting them free from bondage to their sins, healing their sickness of body and mind, stilling the storms that beat upon their souls.

The writers of the New Testament interpret the Cross as the greatest rescue operation in history. In it they see God himself coming to do battle with all the forces of evil, suffering and death which hold man in helpless captivity. They see

[1] *Guideposts*, September 1966.

H

God breaking the power of those forces and setting man free to rise to his full stature of manhood and achieve his destiny as a son of God. That is the theology of the Cross. The experience of the Cross is helpless man kneeling at Calvary, looking up into the face of the Crucified and feeling within himself a sense of liberating power that makes him equal to every crisis and every challenge of life. That can be *your* experience at the Cross and it will stir up within you such a mighty impulse to praise the rescuing God, that you will want to cry out with the Old Testament Psalmist: "*O give thanks unto the Lord, for he is good: for his mercy endureth for ever.*"

GOD ANSWERS

The young man sat in my vestry, lighted a cigarette and stared at me defiantly. "You understand," he said, "that I'm here only to please my mother. She is worried because I won't go to church any more and because I don't believe what I'm supposed to believe." "Yes," I replied, "your mother has spoken to me about it." "Well, it doesn't matter what you say," he blurted. "I've heard all the arguments and read books and I still can't believe." "Books and arguments won't give you back your lost faith," I said. "You need something else." "What's that?" he asked. I replied, "You need the experience of one answered prayer."

This is exactly what many people need. The young doubter was not unique, though he probably thought of himself as such. Belief comes hard to many of us these days. We live in a chilling climate of cynicism which robs religion of its reality and breaks our hold on God. Books will not balance our doubts, because with most of us the trouble is not that we are intellectually impoverished but that we are spiritually starved. What we need is not academic argument but experience; genuine, first-hand, personal religious experience. The experience of one answered prayer might be enough to dispel all our doubts and turn our cynicism to praise.

So it happened to the man who wrote the *116th Psalm.* "I love the Lord", he cries out, and he discloses the reason for this outburst of affectionate praise. "*I love the Lord, because he hath heard my voice and my supplications. Because he hath inclined his ear unto me, therefore will I call upon him as long as I live.*" Then follows a spiritual autobiography in which the Psalmist tells us that he had been ill, agonizingly ill, and had nearly died. From the depths of his pain and weakness he prayed for God's help, and God in his mercy and grace answered him. The almighty God turned heaven's energies on this one lowly creature and restored him to health. A sublime faith now fills the Psalmist's heart. After what God has done for him he can trust God serenely all his days. He feels not only faith but love and obedience. The cynicism engendered by his pain now turns to an exuberant mood of praise, and he does not know how to express his gratitude to God. One thing is sure: he will make it a public act; he will go to church and pay his vows in the presence of the congregation. He wants to share with all the world his tremendous spiritual experience; he wants all men to know how available is the power of God to those who call upon him in their need.

Here, then, was the unshakeable basis of the Psalmist's radiant faith. He discovered that the God of man's experience is *a God who hears and answers prayer*. That is what many of us need to discover if we seriously want to deal with our doubts and turn our cynicism into a mood of praise. If we could look into our lives and point to one specific instance of answered prayer we should have a basis of faith in God that no new knowledge and no battering circumstances can shake. The experience of answered prayer must be our own, but we can be helped by another person's experience. We can study the 116th Psalm, read between the lines and try to infer what was special about this Psalmist that God should hear and answer his prayer.

To begin with, *he did pray*. Consciously, deliberately he presented his need to God and unashamedly asked God to help him. He did not comfort himself with the arrogant attitude, "God knows my condition and he knows what is best for me and he will cure me or let me die. My prayers won't change anything." The Psalmist was too desperate for that. "*I found trouble and sorrow*," he writes, "*Then called I upon the name of the Lord.*"

In a memorable sermon entitled "Does God Read His Children's Mail?" a preacher refers to those immature parents who will stoop to any guile to control their children and will even lift their personal letters from the desk drawer and read them. Now what if God, asks this preacher, is too much of a gentleman for that sort of thing? What if he is too honourable a Father ever to steam open some sealed flap of our thinking, ever to take some thin envelope of our minds and hold it up against the light of his eternal vigilance? What if God, even though he could, simply refuses to read our letters unless they bear his name and address?

It raises the question: When did you last send a letter to God, bearing his name and address? When did you last communicate with him directly concerning some specific need in your life? Imagine yourself in the Psalmist's position. Your health has broken down, you suffer constantly, you are losing weight, you feel yourself becoming weaker day by day. You have consulted your doctor and made the round of specialists, but none seem able to cure you or to do more than prescribe drugs which afford a measure of relief from your distress. In your bitterness of spirit you shake your fist at heaven, crying out rebelliously, "Why has God allowed this to happen to me? What have I done to deserve it?" But why blame God? Have you really brought him into your experience? Have you prayed to him and told him specifically what you want him to do? Have you called upon the name of the Lord?

Isaac Watts defined prayer as "that converse which God hath allowed us to maintain with himself while we are here below . . . that language wherein a creature holds correspondence with his Creator . . ." Prayer is our means of communication with God, but the lines of communication have to be kept open. It is told that, on the night when the *Titanic* sank, the gay passengers had been jamming the wireless with senseless messages to friends in Britain and America. The tragic result was that other ships in the area could not get through to the *Titanic* with their iceberg warnings. It is a parable of our lives which are so often jammed with trivial and frivolous words that the saving Word of God cannot get through to us. If ever we could clear the channels of communication and establish through prayer a direct line with God, God might answer us so clearly and decisively as to dispel our doubts and give us the assurance that we long for.

We can infer that the writer of the 116th Psalm *expected God to answer his prayer*. He does not suggest that, lying on his sick-bed in a weakened condition, he prayed simply as a form of spiritual therapy which boosted his morale and enabled him to endure his suffering with courage and cheerfulness. He wanted to be healed and he told God that he wanted to be healed because he believed that God could heal him. His prayer was a prayer of faith and, because it was a prayer of faith, God answered him.

That could suggest a reason why many of us have never known the experience of answered prayers. Perhaps we have not believed that God will or can do for us what we cannot do for ourselves, and this has made our praying futile, because, unless we have faith, the power of God can no more be discharged into our lives than electricity can be discharged into a non-conductor. Jesus did great things for people during his earthly ministry. He opened their blind eyes, mended their broken bodies, restored use to their wasted limbs, gave sanity to their deranged minds and peace to their troubled souls, but always on one condition—they must have faith. Not that he was the kind of faith-healer who throws the onus on his patients, but he did require that men believe in him and trust him to help them. His constant question of an invalid who sought his help was, "Do you believe that I can do this?" Nor did he demand a large, robust, adventurous faith. Even a tiny timid, tentative faith, if it were humble and sincere, would open the door of a human life to his God-given power.

Faith opens our eyes to the fact that God *is* answering many of our prayers. Again let us put ourselves in the Psalmist's position. Most of us, when we are ill and pray to God for healing, expect that his power will operate miraculously beyond the resources of medical science. We throw up a false distinction between medical healing and divine healing. If we could grasp the truth that all healing is divine, that the power of God operates through the normal channels of medicine and surgery, we might realize that God is, in fact, dealing with us in our condition and that the constant referrals to specialists and the prescription of new drugs are his means of getting us well again. A friend of mine, who is a distinguished Harley Street psychiatrist, often tells a patient, "I cannot cure you. God alone can make you well. He may use me as the instrument of healing." If we looked for God *within* our situation, rather than only expecting him to intervene from *beyond* our situation, we might know that in many marvellous ways God is answering our prayers, and this knowledge would give us a new and unshakeable basis of faith.

The Psalmist *prayed for the healing of his whole personality*. After telling of his distress he says, "*Then called I upon the name of the Lord, O Lord, I beseech thee, deliver my soul.*" A strange prayer, inasmuch as he had obviously been ill in his body. Why did he pray for his soul? Was he just being pious? Had he given up hope? Or did he suspect that his illness, like many organic illnesses, had a spiritual cause—guilt, perhaps, or resentment or frustration—that must be isolated and dealt with before its physical symptoms could be brought under control? There is also the fact that Hebrew thought recognizes no dualism between the body and soul. It sees a man in his totality. If a man lives, the whole man lives; if he dies, the whole man dies. Man is a single being in life and in death; and to pray, "O Lord, I beseech thee, deliver my soul," is to pray not simply for spiritual salvation but for the saving of the whole personality.

One of the significant advances in modern medicine has been the rediscovery of the wholeness of human personality. The name "psychosomatic", applied to medical practice, derives from two Greek words which mean "mind" and "body", and it works on the premise that in any illness the two are inter-dependent and that both must be treated if there is to be a complete cure. Jesus followed that principle. In ministering to human ills he always treated the whole personality. His constant concern was not simply to cleanse the skin or open the eyes or revitalize the legs or straighten the back but to restore the sick person to wholeness and health of body, mind and spirit. He might cure a man's physical symptoms or he might not cure them, but always he brought the saving power of God into a man's situation and healed the man himself.

That is why we can make bold to say that God answers prayer, and not always with a straight "Yes" or "No". God may deny the form of our desires, yet grant us the substance of our needs. Though he does not always answer a man's petitions, always he answers the man himself. The Apostle Paul had to live and work with "a thorn in his flesh". The *New English Bible* calls it "a sharp pain". It was some kind of chronic low-grade illness or physical handicap that made him miserable and put a brake on his activities. Paul tells us that three times he implored God to set him free from this tyrant of pain, and three times he heard God saying to him, "My grace is sufficient for you, for my power is made perfect in weakness" (R.S.V.). That was God's answer. God did not make life easier for Paul but he did promise him the spiritual resources equal to life's demands. He did not remove the nagging thorn in the flesh of his servant but he did help him to make the best of the thorn and to let it make the best of him. God did not answer Paul's petition but he did answer Paul himself.

People whose faith in God rests upon the unshakeable basis of answered prayer are the people, who like the Psalmist, have prayed for the healing of the whole personality. What that means can be seen in the experience of an incurable arthritic who told the hospital chaplain that she found a source of serenity and courage in these words:

> "I asked God for strength, that I might do greater things,
> I was made weak, that I might learn humbly to obey . . .
> I asked for health, that I might do greater things,
> I was given infirmity, that I might do better things . . .
> I asked for riches, that I might be happy,
> I was given poverty, that I might be wise . . .
> I asked for power, that I might have the praise of men,
> I was given weakness, that I might feel the need of God . . .
> I asked for all things, that I might enjoy life,
> I was given life, that I might enjoy all things . . .
> I got nothing that I asked for—but everything I had hoped for,
> Almost despite myself, my unspoken prayers were answered,
> I am among all men, most richly blessed."[1]

The Psalmist *prayed out of a total relationship with God.* That is what we infer from his reaction to the gift of healing—which was not a dismissal of God until he needed him again but a grateful resolve to live close to God in the worship of God's house and the life of religious devotion. Presumably this had been the pattern of his life before his critical illness. Presumably he had always tried to live close to God, so that, when he brought his desperate situation into God's presence, he was not walking on unfamiliar ground. With the Psalmist prayer was not a neon-marked emergency exit to be taken only in time of calamity when all the other exits are blocked. Communion with God was the normal habit of his life. Therefore, when he prayed to God in a time of crisis he was spiritually conditioned to receive an answer from God and to recognize it as such.

---

[1] These words of an unknown Confederate soldier can be seen cast in bronze in the lobby of the Institute of Physical Medicine and Rehabilitation in New York City.

If it has never seemed to us that God has answered our prayers, the reason could be that we have not been spiritually conditioned to receive and recognize an answer. We have not prayed often enough, long enough and hard enough. We have not brought our lives into harmony with God's purpose. Jesus taught his disciples to pray without ceasing. "He spake a parable unto them to this end, that men ought always to pray, and not to faint"; and the parable recorded a woman's tiresome, reiterating petitioning of a judge, so that finally out of sheer exasperation he dealt with her case. In this parable the judge stands in contrast to God, not in similarity with him, and the lesson is: If it was worth while praying persistently to the unjust judge, how much more worth while praying persistently to the Father God. Some prayers God cannot answer overnight. Some things God cannot or will not give us until we are spiritually conditioned to receive them, and prayer is the spiritual discipline that conditions us.

In one of his many helpful books Dr. Roger Pilkington tells of an experience which happened to him some years ago. He had gone to South Wales to give a series of lectures in a postgraduate biology course. Through a succession of unforeseen events he was forced to change his hotel. When he finally arrived at the place where he was to stay for the night, a tired-looking and pale middle-aged receptionist greeted him. "We can only get you a cold supper," she said. "But if you come into the office any time after nine o'clock you can have a cup of tea."

Dr. Pilkington lectured that evening and, when he returned to the hotel, he decided to accept the offer of a cup of tea. He found the receptionist chatting with two commercial travellers and discussing, oddly enough, the subject of suicide. Thinking him a medical doctor, she asked him if he thought that people who put their heads in a gas oven suffered a lot of pain. She also asked if he knew how many aspirin tablets would make up a lethal dose. The conversation switched to less morbid subjects, and Dr. Pilkington, finishing his tea, retired for the night.

But he could not sleep. He had been lying wide-awake in bed for a few moments when a feeling came over him which he describes as "a sense of being charged like a condenser". Throwing on his dressing gown, he ran down four flights of stairs, walked straight into the inner office, confronted the receptionist and asked bluntly, "I want to know why you are going to commit suicide." She began to protest, but Dr. Pilkington cut her short. "I know you're going to. I shall not stop you. But you must tell me *why* you are going to do it?" The woman broke down and told him her story. At the age of forty-three her father had become totally blind, and she, who was now approaching her forty-third birthday, had been told in all sincerity by the family doctor that the disease was hereditary. Unable to face the thought of a lonely spinsterhood of helpless blindness, she had decided to opt out of life by committing suicide. It happened that in those days Dr. Pilkington was a geneticist and that he had been working on eye defects in animals and had also made a particular study of the inheritance of faults of vision in humans. The receptionist had only to describe her father's condition in the barest outline for him to see at once that it was not hereditary. He convinced her of this beyond a shadow of a doubt. "You can go back to bed," she said, "I know you are not deceiving me. Don't worry. I shall not kill myself tonight or ever." She also told him that every day since consulting her doctor she had prayed the same prayer "Please God, show me how I can kill myself and put an end to it all."[1]

What do you call it—coincidence? It hardly seems so when you put all the factors together, especially the two major factors —a desperate woman praying for help, and the one man who combined the scientific knowledge and Christian sympathy to meet her need. "The whole thing," writes Dr. Pilkington, "had that peculiar brilliant simplicity which one never fails to encounter when dealing with the works of God." It was the 116th Psalm all over again, a demonstration in terms of real life that the God with whom we have to do is a God who hears and answers prayer. Never again will that hotel receptionist doubt what God can do for her. When a person has prayed passionately and persistently to God and is convinced that God has heard and answered him, he has a foundation for faith that no force of argument or cruel circumstance can ever shake. Belief in God comes hard these days, but the experience of one answered prayer would be enough to dispel all our doubts and turn all our cynicism to praise.

[1] Roger Pilkington, *Heavens Alive* (Macmillan and Co. Ltd., London, 1964), pp. 120–5.

GOD VINDICATES

The picture is that of a great building—a university, a cathedral, a library or a court of justice—rising from its foundations. The contractor inspects a load of quarried stone which has just been delivered. Some stones he approves, a few he rejects. Later in the day the architect arrives on the scene to survey the growing structure and sees a small heap of discarded stones piled on the edge of the site. One stone catches his attention, and he examines it closely. He has never seen anything so flawless. It will make the perfect corner-stone. Calling the contractor, he asks, "Why have you rejected this one?" The builder replies, "It doesn't fit in with the others." "Then the others must be chiselled to fit in with this one," says the architect. So the stone which the builders refused is polished, inscribed and set in the place of honour; it becomes the head stone of the corner.

That could be a parable of Jesus. Actually it was the figure of speech used by an Old Testament Psalmist to describe the activity of God in his life and which caused him to cry out of a full heart, "*O give thanks unto the Lord; for he is good: because his mercy endureth for ever.*" We don't know who wrote the *118th Psalm* or what were his exact circumstances but we can quickly infer from the Psalm itself that the author had been tossed aside like an unwanted stone, alone and rejected. As a king or a military leader he had been betrayed by his allies and smothered by his enemies. "*They compassed me about like bees,*" he writes. With every man's hand against him he nevertheless stood his ground, believing it "*better to trust in the Lord than to put confidence in princes.*" His trust was not ill-founded, because in the end God came to his rescue. "*I called upon the Lord in distress: the Lord answered me, and set me in a large place.*" God vindicated his faithful servant, championed his cause, gave him victory over his enemies and proved him right in the eyes of all his people. Thus he describes his personal triumph: "*The stone which the builders refused is become the head stone of the corner. This is the Lord's doing; it is marvellous in our eyes."*

The Old Testament Psalms anticipate the whole of the Christian Gospel. Somewhere in the Hebrew Psalter you will find foregleams of all the great doctrines of the Christian Faith. Every season of the Church Year has its appropriate Psalms. At Advent we look forward, with the writer of the 72nd Psalm, to the coming of a King who "shall have dominion also from sea to sea, and from the river unto the ends of the earth." At Christmas we sing the words of Psalm 24: "Lift up your heads, O ye gates; even lift them up, ye everlasting doors; and the King of glory shall come in". During Lent we recite many Psalms that express our penitence; and on Good Friday we read from the 22nd Psalm words that came as a cry from the Cross: "My God, my God, why hast thou forsaken me?" On Ascension Day we express our joy with the writer of Psalm 47: "God is gone up with a shout, the Lord with the sound of a trumpet"; and at Pentecost we pray to the inescapable God in the words of the 139th Psalm, "Whither shall I go from thy spirit . . .?" On Easter Day Christian people in countless churches throughout the world chant the 118th Psalm, the great, familiar song of Easter which declares, *"This is the day which the Lord hath made; we will rejoice and be glad in it."*

The 118th Psalm belongs to Easter because it could so easily have come from the lips of Jesus himself; it could have been his song of triumph when he emerged from the darkness of the tomb. On the night before his Crucifixion Jesus withdrew to the Garden of Gethsemane where he pleaded with God that, if it were possible, the cup of suffering might pass from him. In obedience to God's will he drank the cup of suffering to its bitter dregs. Suppose that at the end of the first Easter Day, after appearing to the women in the garden, the despondent pair on the Emmaus Road and the eleven scared disciples in the Upper Room, the Risen Christ had returned to Gethsemane, what would have been his prayer then? Surely such words as these:

"The Lord is my strength and song, and is become my salvation . . . The right hand of the Lord is exalted: the right hand of the Lord doeth valiantly. I shall not die, but live, and declare the works of the Lord. The Lord hath chastened me

sore: but he hath not given me over unto death . . . The stone which the builders refused is become the head stone of the corner. This is the Lord's doing; it is marvellous in our eyes."

One tremendous truth emerges from the 118th Psalm when we lift it from the Old Testament and set it in the larger context of Easter. It is the truth that the God and Father of our Lord Jesus Christ has demonstrated to all the world that he is *a God who vindicates.* This was the initial truth of Christ's Resurrection that laid hold on the disciples and turned their sadness into joy and altered their horizons and changed the complexion of their whole world. For eighteen months they had followed the Teacher of Nazareth, confident that God was with him and that the way of life which he taught and exemplified was the way that God intended all men to live. But most men rejected Jesus, they compassed him about like bees, they said that he didn't fit into the social structure, so they broke his body and tossed him aside like an unwanted stone. On Good Friday his few faithful followers felt like fools for having pinned their hopes to a life that could so easily be snuffed out like a candle by the winds of evil and brute force and hypocrisy. No, his was not the right way; obviously it had no future. Then came Easter Sunday and with it a radical about-face in their thinking. The fires of hope now burned with inextinguishable brightness, because now the disciples knew that, by raising Jesus from the dead, God had vindicated him, championed his cause, given him victory over his enemies and proved him right in the eyes of all his people.

When you read the earliest Christian sermons in the Acts of the Apostles you discover that this is primarily what Easter meant to the followers of Jesus. Declaring himself to be a witness to the Resurrection, Peter on the Day of Pentecost said to a great congregation of Jews, "Let all the house of Israel therefore know assuredly that God has made him both Lord and Christ, this Jesus whom you crucified". In the minds of the apostles it was the Resurrection that proved Jesus to be the Son of God with power and validated their conviction and the claims which he himself had made that he was God's Messiah. If Jesus had rotted in the tomb he might have been remembered as a great historical figure, a wise teacher, "the man for others", as many liberals are satisfied to designate him today, but that would be all. There would be no Gospel, no Church, no New Testament. What created the Gospel, what gave birth to the Church and what bound the disciples in ever-lasting loyalty to Christ as Lord and Master was the burning belief, attested by their own eyes, that God had raised Christ from the tomb and eternally vindicated his way for men.

The Apostle Paul takes up the same theme in his *Letter to the Philippians*. Pleading for a spirit of love and humility among his friends at Philippi, Paul exhorts them as Christians to have "the mind of Christ" who, though he was essentially and eternally God, gave up the glory of his Divinity to take upon him our humanity, taking the lowest form of humanity, that of a slave to God and his fellow-men and, in obedience to God, suffering the most disgraceful of deaths, death on a cross. "So much," sneers the cynic, "for the way of humility and love! Did not men totally reject it? Did they not utterly annihilate it?" Yet we call Jesus "Lord". Why? Not because he left behind him a shining example or a deathless philosophy, not because future generations made him immortal, but be-cause God accepted his obedience and vindicated him. "There-fore," shouts Paul, "God has highly exalted him and bestowed on him the name which is above every name, that at the name of Jesus every knee should bow, in heaven and on earth and under the earth, and every tongue confess that Jesus Christ is Lord, to the glory of God the Father". Men showed what they thought of Jesus by putting him to death. God showed what he thought of Jesus by raising him from the dead.

In the great fifteenth chapter of his *First Letter to the Corin-thians* Paul takes this thought a step further and relates it to our situation. He sees Christ not only as an historical figure, not only as a man, but as the Man whom God gave to represent a new beginning for the human race. The first representative man was Adam who died; and, since we are all by natural birth sons of Adam, we shall all die. Christ is the Second Adam whom God raised from the dead; and, since by spiritual rebirth we can identify ourselves with Christ, we therefore have hope that God will also raise us from the dead. Paul writes, "For as in Adam all die, even so in Christ shall all be made alive." What happened to Christ may happen to us, if we are "in Christ". As God vindicated his obedience, so we have hope that God will vindicate our obedience. On this note of exultant hope Paul concludes his Resurrection Symphony: "Therefore, my beloved brethren, be ye steadfast, unmoveable, always abounding in the work of the Lord, forasmuch as ye know that your labour is not in vain in the Lord."

This is surely a Word of God that every Christian needs to hear. It has never been easy to lead a life committed to Christ's way of humility and love. The world crucified it once and the world has been crucifying it ever since. When we think of the forces that aligned themselves against Jesus and compassed him about like bees—the vested interests of the priests, the moral cowardice of Pontius Pilate, the brute force of the Roman soldiers, the callous indifference of the gawking spectators—does it not seem that these are the very forces that smother the spirit of Christ in every good man today? What chance does a Christian have against them?

For some Christians the issue becomes intensely real and personal. I remember talking with an employer who confessed with deep despondency that he found it very difficult these days not to become embittered. He was not the super-religious type but he was a deeply committed Christian of the old-fashioned variety who tried to practise the teachings of Jesus and who consistently asked himself in every situation, "What does Jesus want me to do?" Like his father before him he took a personal interest in his employees and tried to treat them fairly and generously but he found that the men were no longer interested in this benevolent relationship. Before ever he could anticipate their needs, a pair of tough union negotiators would be seated in front of his desk, demanding all that he intended to give and much more besides. His competitors, whom he once regarded as friends, now appeared as conspirators, plotting to take him over and put him out of business. This man felt like a social anachronism. "I guess I'm behind the times," he observed sadly. "What really disturbs me is the thought that these people may be right, and I may have been wrong all the time."

Every sensitive Christian has come to terms with that issue. In the world today we can see two ways of life locked together in a life-and-death struggle: on the one hand, the way of vested interest, moral cowardice, brute force and callous indifference; on the other hand, the way of unselfish service, moral courage, tender pity and suffering love; the way of Christ and the way of anti-Christ. Which way is right? Which will win out? Which pays off? There can be no doubt in the constricted minds of people who take a frog's-eye view of life and the world. They cry out, "To hell with all this silly sentiment about love and humility. Assert your rights, grab what you can and let the other fellow look out for himself!" For a time it may seem that they are right. To the soldiers who arrested him in Gethsemane Jesus said, "This is your hour." Brutality, selfishness, compromise, indifference always have their hour. But such a short, fleeting hour!

There is another view of life and the world. Without wanting to be irreverent we may describe it as a God's-eye view. It is a way of looking at life in the light of all that we know of God's activity in human experience, of the kind of God that he is and of all that he has done and promised to do. The event of Easter confirms the experience of a Hebrew Psalmist who found him to be a God who vindicates. It declares that God has once and for all pronounced his verdict on the struggle that rages within and among men. By raising Christ from the dead God has demonstrated decisively and conclusively that in his world the only way of life that will have any future is the way of Christ, the way of unselfish service, moral courage, tender pity and suffering love. Easter means that when God makes visible in Jesus a way of life that he wants us to follow he does not promise that it will pay off in terms of the world's rewards but he does promise that ultimately he will vindicate us as he vindicated Jesus.

A dramatic example of God's vindication in our time concerns the great Catholic theologian, Pierre Teilhard de Chardin. Born in 1881, he entered the Jesuit order at age seventeen and was ordained a priest in 1911. Except for the First World War, in which he served on the front line as a non-combatant stretcher-bearer, winning three medals for bravery under fire, Teilhard devoted his life to the study of science. Throughout his career he wrote several books on theology from a scientific point of view, but the Roman Church suspected him for it, and his superiors sent him to the Far East in a kind of "banishment". Not one of his books was allowed to be published during his lifetime. Even as late as 1962, seven years after his death, an official warning was issued against the heresy thought to be inherent in his writings. Teilhard accepted these rebuffs with complete loyalty and obedience, though never compromising his position, always believing that, if he was right, God would prove him right. It seems that God *has* proved him right. God has vindicated his obedient servant. Prominent on any bookstall, Protestant or Catholic, today you will find the published translated works of Teilhard de Chardin. Theologians of all traditions acclaim them as "epoch-making". Some see in Teilhard another Thomas Aquinas, the great, authentic interpreter of Christianity to the mind of this age. Truly "the stone which the builders refused is become the head stone of the corner. This is the Lord's doing; it is marvellous in our eyes."

The Easter Psalm speaks a heartening Word of God to all men and women with a social conscience who are actively concerned with promoting the Christian way of life in society. It is in the social arena that the struggle rages most fiercely, and to Christians it often seems like a losing struggle, because Christ is crucified in our common life by the very forces that crucified him on the Hill of Calvary He is crucified by sheer pessimism like that of an Englishman who said after the Second World War, after the blitz, the destruction and the loss of life, "One thing is sure, the Christian religion has 'had it' in this country. We have tried to set an example to the world. We have tried to help other countries and give moral leadership, but where has it got us? We have tried the so-called way of Christ. Well, obviously that way doesn't work!"

As gently as possible we have to ask that man, "What way does work? The way of anti-Christ, the way of vested interest, moral cowardice, brute force and callous indifference—will *that* work for the building of a stronger country and a better world?" It is told that an assistant of Thomas Edison once tried to console the inventor over the failure of a series of experiments. "It is too bad," he said, "to do all that work without any results." "Oh," replied Mr. Edison, "we have lots of results. We know seven hundred things that won't work." By this time we ought to know a great many things that won't work in our world. We know that the prodigious expenditures to put men on other planets will not work to put

I

food into the empty stomachs of the exploding population in underdeveloped areas on this planet. We know that the killing in Far Eastern countries and the competitive armament race will not work to bring peace to peoples who have tasted nothing but war since the day of their birth. We know that high walls and barbed-wired fences and obsolescent racial policies will not work to bring peoples of different skin colours and ideologies into closer understanding and co-operation. We know that labour disputes that cause innocent people to suffer will not work to create a social order of justice and equality. We know that gambling and drunkenness and L.S.D. and a culture saturated with sex will not work to lift the human race to a level of dignity and nobility.

When we ask of Christ's way, "Does it work?" we are dealing not with a theory but with a fact of history. What has, in fact, worked in the sense that it has changed the world for the better and removed man further from his origins in the slime and brought him nearer to the fulfilment of his human destiny? In the early centuries of this era it was the zeal of the the apostles who threw their frail bodies against the invincible might of Rome and broke themselves in order to break down the stone wall of a dehumanizing social order. In the Dark Ages the monasteries were among the most potent factors in civilization—brave, flickering candles of faith that prevented the darkness from becoming total darkness. In the Middle Ages the Protestant Reformation gave to the world a new kind of religious freedom that became the basis of modern democracy. In eighteenth-century England an evangelical revival sparked off a passion for social reform that swept the length and breadth of the land like a prairie fire and saved it from a bloody revolution as grim and ghastly as that taking place in France. In modern times Christian missionaries, teaching and healing in the Name of Christ, have given the peoples of other nations a sense of belonging, a sense of selfhood, a realization of their own worth and dignity in the sight of God. Human lives, controlled by the spirit of Christ and dedicated to the service of Christ—these have worked to build a better world, not because they were great and influential but because God vindicated them.

Towards the close of the eighteenth century a small group of Christian politicians, headed by William Wilberforce, introduced in the British Parliament a bill to abolish the slave trade. Despite strong and bitter opposition, victory seemed certain; but it happened that on the evening when the bill was being read for the third time, a comic opera opened in London. While a dozen of Wilberforce's sure supporters were swelling the applause for a popular singer of the day, the slave trade seized the opportunity provided by their absence and in a depleted House threw out the bill by a vote of 74 to 70. "I am personally hurt," said Wilberforce. To which some of his friends replied, "Why don't you give up? You can't win anyway!" But Wilberforce did not give up. He refused to be intimidated by opposition or indifference. His supporters were few, but he held stubbornly to the belief that numbers do not count in the struggle for social righteousness. What counts is the support of God. Public opinion seemed to prove him wrong, but he had faith that he was right and that, if he was right, God would prove him right. In the end God did prove him right. God vindicated this faithful follower of Christ, as he will vindicate every servant of the common good, raising him from the grave of human scorn to the resurrection life of man's eternal gratitude.

God's vindication of Jesus did not end with the appearance of the Risen Christ to his disciples on the first Easter Day. That was only the beginning. Twenty centuries of lived experience have placed their seal of approval on the way of life that Jesus taught and exemplified in ancient Palestine. Even George Bernard Shaw, that brilliant, heretical Irishman, who not only saw through many of the shams of modern life but who looked deeply into some of its ultimate needs, once wrote:

"I am no more Christian than Pilate was, or you, gentle reader, and yet, like Pilate, I greatly prefer Jesus to Annas or Caiaphas, and I am ready to assert that, after contemplating the world and human nature for many years, I see no way out of the world's misery but the way which would have been found by Christ's will if he had undertaken the work of a modern practical statesman."

But this is faint praise, because we know that Christ is something far greater than a modern practical statesman. He is the living Son of God who even now makes known his will for our lives and for the structure of society. Men may refuse his will, as they refused it long ago, they may toss it aside like an unwanted stone; but because God raised Jesus from the dead, we shall continue to struggle for his way of life, believing that the stone which the builders refuse will become the head stone of the corner. This will be the Lord's doing, and it will be marvellous in our eyes.

GOD UNIFIES

For several years in England I had my hair cut regularly by a barber who was a convinced Communist. He was a decent fellow and an efficient barber but he cut hair only to earn a living. The main purpose of his life was to preach the gospel according to Karl Marx. The moment he had a customer trapped in his chair this zealous Figaro began to talk, waxing eloquent against the evils of a capitalist society. He verbally scourged the Christian Church, never directly to me but always to other customers in my presence. Eventually he became so unreasonable and offensive that I couldn't stand it any longer, so one day I walked out of his shop and took my patronage to another barber, an older man who proudly said that he voted for the Conservative Party.

The first man was not a sinister character. Indeed, his zeal for Communism may have been a tribute to his own greatness as a human being. Man cannot live by bread or by barbering alone. Every man needs something bigger to live for—a philosophy, an ideal, a goal that unifies his personality and gives meaning to his life; and my obnoxious friend found that cohesive force in Communism. He took pleasure in his private crusade, he enjoyed it, so much, in fact, that when I asked him if he couldn't cut hair more quietly, he replied that if he were not allowed to talk while he worked he would give up barbering. Communism gave him moral purpose, a sense of living not for himself alone but for all the underdogs of society and for the building of a better world. Communism comforted him; it compensated for all the disadvantages, real or imaginary, which he as one of society's underdogs had always suffered. Communism gave him a source of hope. He had been to Russia and he saw the Russian way of life as a great tidal wave of social justice that would inexorably cover the earth as the waters cover the sea. An insignificant barber cutting hair six days a week in a dingy basement shop! Who can blame him for embracing a philosophy that drew together all the divergent trends of his life and made him, as he thought, a complete personality?

Yet it was sad that this son of Abraham turned to an atheist social theory, because he could have found a more permanent and satisfying philosophy in his own rich religious heritage. On every page of the Old Testament he could have met his racial ancestors, no less underprivileged than himself, who believed in God and whose religious faith acted as a unifying force that gave meaning to their little lives. One of them is the writer of the *119th Psalm,* a Hebrew poet who brought God into his experience and discovered that he is above all *a God who unifies.*

John Ruskin, writing of those portions of the Bible which he had been made to memorize in boyhood, says, "That which cost me most to learn, and which was to my child's view, chiefly repulsive—the 119th Psalm—has now become of all the most precious to me." This is the longest of the Psalms (176 verses in all) and it should be savoured slowly and at intervals rather than at one sitting, else the reader will suffer a case of mental indigestion. Fortunately the intervals are well-defined. The Psalm is set in the form of an acrostic. There are twenty-two stanzas corresponding to the twenty-two letters in the Hebrew alphabet. Each stanza has eight lines, and each line begins with the same Hebrew letter. In the English equivalent it would mean that each of the eight lines of the first stanza begins with the letter A, each line in the second begins with B, and so on through the alphabet.

But we mustn't be bored or even too fascinated by this artificial arrangement. The Psalmist was not an old-fashioned preacher using a homoletical gimmick which eclipsed the content of his message. He was a great poet possessed by a great truth and he employed the best literary device in order to impress that truth upon his readers. It was not just an academic truth either, but the constitutive principle of his life, the basic philosophy that drew the divergent trends of his personality together and made him a complete human being. A single theme runs through this longest of the Psalms. That theme is God's Law, variously expressed as God's statutes, precepts, commandments, testimonies, word, ways and judgments. The Psalmist has brought God into his experience, and God has given him, among other blessings, a Law that unifies his little life around a single philosophy and gives it meaning and purpose. We may conjecture that if the Communist barber had ever met the writer of the 119th Psalm he might never have felt the need to meet Karl Marx.

The Psalmist would tell him that there is *pleasure in keeping God's Law*.

"Blessed are the undefiled in the way, who walk in the law of the Lord. Blessed are they that keep his testimonies, and that seek him with the whole heart."

The rest of the Psalm is a prayer and, as such, it tells us more about the author than we could learn if he spoke directly to us. This Hebrew poet has found God's Law to be such a never-failing source of delight and happiness and joy in his life that he proclaims his gladness not to man but to God. He thanks God out of a full heart:

"O how I love thy law! it is my meditation all the day . . . thy law is my delight . . . Thy testimonies are wonderful . . . Thy statutes have been my songs in the house of my pilgrimage . . . I have rejoiced in the way of thy testimonies, as much as in all riches . . . The law of thy mouth is better unto me than thousands of gold and silver . . . The righteousness of thy testimonies is everlasting: give me understanding, and I shall live . . ."

There are some people who might raise an eyebrow at this man's enthusiasm for God's Law. "An odd sort of character," they say. "Probably a fanatical legalist. What normal person actually takes pleasure in keeping laws?" Most of us believe that laws are necessary and good for the well-being of society and we observe them because we have to, not always because we want to. Ever since we were children at school, governed by the rules of the classroom, we have regarded laws as the compulsive and restrictive element in life which it was fun to throw off from time to time. Ever since Adam and Eve men and women have rebelled against the laws of God, believing that there was greater pleasure in freedom from those laws than in being bound by them. Our generation has reacted quite vehemently against God's laws, a reaction sanctified by modern moralists and by some theologians who claim that there is no such thing as a fixed code of human behaviour laid down by a Supranatural God and applicable to every situation. Some would go further and say that there is no such thing as a Supranatural God. How does this double denial affect man in his search for the pleasure and happiness that will give meaning to his life?

Canadians recall the furore in the press and Parliament caused by a popular television programme in the autumn of 1966. It consisted partly of a film, produced in Britain, which showed a young man and woman, on more than friendly terms, occupying the same bed and discussing in a desultory manner whether they wanted to get married. An unseen interviewer then spoke to each of them separately and asked some shockingly intimate questions about their rather promiscuous sex life. The programme raised a chorus of protests from indignant taxpayers who resented this publicly-financed garbage being dumped into their living rooms. Strangely enough, there were no protests against another feature of the same programme which showed a live interview with an Episcopalian Bishop whose ventilation of his own doubts and floundering efforts to answer questions indicated that he is well on his way to rejecting the Bible idea of God. Can it be that most viewers failed to see the connection between these two features in the programme? When a man is sure of God, a Creator, Sovereign God who governs the world according to his laws, and when a man loves that God he finds delight and pleasure in living by God's laws. When man rejects the God of Mount Sinai he turns to other delights and pleasures, even those that exploit, pervert and destroy human personality.

One of the big lies being circulated in our day is the spurious claim that the religion of Jesus contains no rules. A school child has only to read the New Testament in order to find out that Jesus stated explicitly that he came not to abrogate the laws of God but to make those same laws more positive, more spiritual and more demanding. What are the Beatitudes if not the laws of the Kingdom of God? Jesus enunciated them not to take pleasure out of life but to put pleasure into it. Each one begins with the word "Blessed", the key-word of the 119th Psalm; and their whole point is precisely that in living by these divinely-given rules of humility, meekness, purity and righteousness, a man will find a unifying philosophy of life that brings him the highest happiness and makes him a complete person.

In God's Law the Psalmist found also a *moral purpose* that gave meaning to his life. Indeed, he impresses me as the one man in the Old Testament who truly incarnates the beatitude of Jesus: "Blessed are they which do hunger and thirst after righteousness." He has one consuming ambition, an insatiable appetite to understand and obey and fulfil the Law of God for his life. Hear how fervently he prays:

"Teach me, O Lord, the way of thy statutes; and I shall keep it unto the end. Give me understanding, and I shall keep thy law; yea, I shall observe it with my whole heart. Make me to go in the path of thy commandments; for therein do I delight. Incline my heart unto thy testimonies, and not to covetousness . . . O that my ways were directed to keep thy statutes . . . Behold, I have longed after thy precepts: quicken me in thy righteousness . . ."

How could such a life fail to have superlative meaning? Nothing does more to draw together the divergent trends of personality and give cohesion to a man's life than the sense of being caught up in some significant purpose. You meet a boy in his late teens who is the despair of his parents and teachers. He is sullen, lazy, uncommunicative. He spends hours locked up in his room listening to inane gramophone records, then he roars off on his motorcycle to join the gang, looking as untidy as an unwashed and uncombed dog. One day you meet him again and you scarcely recognize him as the same person. He has had his hair cut, he wears conventional clothes, he talks seriously and intelligently and gives the impression that he knows where he is going. The truth is that he does know where he is going. He has taken an interesting job in a business firm with real prospect of advancement, and all his scattered energies have been drawn together in the single consuming purpose to succeed. Almost in prayer he says to his employers, "Give me understanding, and I shall keep thy law; yea, I shall observe it with my whole heart."

Look at the same person twenty-five years later. He has not yet entered his second childhood but he has certainly reverted to the worst stage of his adolescence. Once he was a youthful delinquent, lazy, unkempt and undisciplined; now he seems to be a middle-aged delinquent, lazy, unkempt and undisciplined. Instead of roaring off on a motorcycle he now roars off in his Cadillac; instead of joining the gang at the street-corner he now joins the gang at the club bar. So far as he knows, his parents don't worry about him any more because they are dead, but his wife sits alone in the evenings and worries herself sick. What has happened to this man whose life was once united around the consuming ambition to succeed?

The answer is that he has achieved his ambition. He has climbed the ladder of success, made money, built the big house and the summer cottage, educated his children, bought all the grown-up toys, and now he feels that he has nothing left to strive for. This is just the tragedy of so many lives. Where fruition should set in, strain and stagnation set in. They collapse at the half-way mark, because the goals and purposes of youth are too small, too weak and too limited to sustain them past middle-age. It needs larger goals and a more enduring purpose to give life a permanent meaning.

Some men have found that enduring purpose in the Law of God. Once it was my privilege to spend half an hour in the home of Karl Barth, chatting informally with the great theologian. He was seventy-two years of age at the time, and I innocently asked if he planned to bring out any more volumes of his monumental *Dogmatics*. He laughed with youthful vigour and replied, "Of course! And when I complete the doctrinal works I shall go on to Christian ethics." Barth spoke in a larger sense than he realized. Christian ethics are always ahead of us, even at the age of seventy-two, and not only as an academic study but as the enduring purpose of God for our lives. No man ever reaches the point where he can cease to pray, "Give me understanding, and I shall keep thy law; yea, I shall observe it with my whole heart." The one purpose that will unify a man's life and give it meaning to the very end— and, we believe, beyond that end—is the creation of moral character.

The Law of God gave the Psalmist *comfort in his affliction*. He tells God that, but for his delight in the Law, he would have perished in his affliction. Even in trouble and anguish he still found pleasure in trying to live by God's commandments.

Indeed, he says that it was good for him to be afflicted so that he might learn God's statutes. The Psalmist does not specify the nature of his affliction, but we gather that it was brought on by powerful enemies who framed him, tried to trap him and lay in wait to kill him. Even princes spoke against him and persecuted him without a cause. The most descriptive passage in the Psalm begins at verse 81 where the author tells God that his soul faints, his eyes fail, he has become like a bottle in the smoke; the proud have digged pits for him, wrongfully persecuted him and almost destroyed him; but he hopes in God's word, he does not forget God's statutes nor forsake God's precepts.

The Psalmist is not boasting; he doesn't pray, like the Pharisee in the temple, with a sense of moral superiority. He has made a choice in life and he believes it to be the right choice. Trouble, sorrow, misfortune, persecution befall every man, especially the man who lives a life of such flawless integrity that it chides lesser men, so that they want to put it out of their sight. Once a Man was crucified for that very reason. Some people, when evil crushes their souls, succumb to it and allow themselves to be dragged down to the level of moral mediocrity which seems to yield the quickest and easiest reward in terms of worldly success and pleasure. Not so the Hebrew Psalmist. The affliction that he suffered and the seeming prosperity of wicked and godless men only hardened him in his resolution to live on the high level of godly integrity. God's Law made him as strong as a rock. It compensated him with the knowledge that he possessed a reward more lasting and satisfying than the perishable pleasures of the world. It even stirred his sympathy for wicked and godless men. The Law of God was his unfailing source of comfort and stability.

Rudyard Kipling's novel *Kim* is the fabulous and enchanting story of an Irish orphan lad brought up in India. To train him for the Secret Service the British army sent him to the home of Lurgan Sahib, a mysterious character skilled in the art of hypnosis. Lurgan put Kim in a trance, gave him an earthen jar and ordered him to throw it on the floor. The jar broke into fifty pieces. "Look at it," whispered Lurgan, "It shall come to life again, piece by piece." Kim could not turn his head. The jar, smashed before his eyes, seemed to be coming together. "Look, it's coming to shape," Lurgan purred. As Kim shook himself, trying to resist the hypnotic spell, his mind took refuge in the multiplication table. "It's coming into shape," Lurgan repeated. "Twice three equals six," Kim said to himself, "and three times three is nine, and four times three is twelve." Kim clung desperately to the repetition. The shadow outline of the jar cleared like a mist lifting. "Three times twelve is thirty-six." "Look, it's coming into shape?" Lurgan's statement was a question. "No, it is smashed," Kim gasped, free from the spell that had almost engulfed his mind.

You see how Kim saved himself. He clung to the truths which he knew were true—two times three is six, and three times three is nine. No matter what illusions threatened to swamp his mind, these things were true and sound; nothing could change them. That is what the Psalmist did, and that is what *we* must do when our minds are confused, and our lives are shattered by suffering and evil, and everything about us seems to challenge all that we have ever believed. We must try to resist the hypnosis of man-made morality and cling for dear life to God's eternal standards of right and wrong enunciated on Mount Sinai and on another mountain beside the Sea of Galilee. We must believe that if we stand by them they will stand by us and give our lives a cohesion and a meaning which no evil and no suffering, real or illusory, can ever destroy.

God's Law gave the Psalmist *a source of hope*. A single phrase keeps recurring in his long, sustained prayer, the phrase, "*according to thy word*". Everything he asks from God—strength, comfort, salvation, mercy—he asks according to God's word. Whenever it refers to God's word the Psalmist's prayer reaches sublime heights of assurance and hope.

"*Thou hast dealt well with thy servant, O Lord, according to thy word . . . Remember thy word unto thy servant, upon which thou hast caused me to hope . . . Thy word is true from the beginning: and every one of thy righteous judgments endureth for ever . . . For ever, O Lord, thy word is settled in heaven . . . Thy word is a lamp unto my feet, and a light unto my path . . .*"

It recalls another phrase, frequently used in our common speech and intended to tell us a great deal about a person—"His word is as good as his bond". Applied to a friend, it means that we can trust what he says; we can rely upon his word as though it were a legal guarantee and stake our lives upon the truth of it. Applied to God, it means that God's Law is backed up by God's Word. The life which God commands us to live and work for here upon earth contains its own promise and guarantee that this life is right, eternally right, and that in the end it will be the only life that prevails and gives meaning to the individual and to society.

I wish that my barber friend, who found his hope in the ultimate triumph of Communism, could have watched a television show, produced a few years ago, that exercised a tremendous impact on public imagination. Its moral power lay in the play within the play. Lounging in a New York bar, a half-drunk intellectual virtually acted out before the other customers a drama which he had written. The scene takes place in the United Nations Building on the eve of World War Three. The great powers have declared war and have set midnight as the zero hour when they will press the ominous buttons that let loose the flames of hell upon earth. Meanwhile, they have agreed to a four-hour truce to allow the world's most able men to assemble for the purpose of testing a computer. According to the inventor this machine, if supplied with man's highest wisdom, can provide the answer that will prevent the human race from stumbling over the edge of chaos. The computer stands in the centre of the council chamber. One by one they come forward—statesmen, educators, militarists, philosophers, poets, economists, journalists, scientists—each pouring into this cold automaton the distilled wisdom of the ages according to his branch of knowledge. But nothing happens. The entire world trembles over Death's chasm, and nothing happens until one minute before midnight. Then, suddenly, the computer shudders and its lights flicker. From its mouth comes a slip of paper which the inventor takes in his hand and reads before the hushed assembly. This is the answer, the supreme wisdom which alone can save civilization from violent suicide: "Thou shalt have no other gods before me . . . Thou shalt not make unto thee any graven image . . . Thou shalt not steal . . . Thou shalt not kill . . . Thou shalt not covet . . ."

How can we be sure that this is in fact the highest wisdom, on which we can depend and in which we can hope for the world's salvation and for our own? We can be sure because, like the Old Testament Psalmist, we have hoped in God's

Word, and because the Word of God, in the sense of God's eternal guarantee, has been fulfilled in the New Testament. The Fourth Gospel begins, "In the beginning was the Word, and the Word was with God, and the Word was God." In this Word "was life, and the life was the light of men. The light shines in the darkness, and the darkness has not overcome it" (R.S.V.). That's what the Gospel story is all about. It tells us that this eternal Word of God "became flesh, and dwelt among us, full of grace and truth". Jesus is the Word of God, the Law of God, the life of God made visible in history, and the darkness has not overcome it. Here on earth he lived that life with clear and lofty grandeur and carried it unhurt through death. His was the one complete life this world has ever known: it combined all the unifying qualities of pleasure, moral purpose, comfort and hope. He gives this complete life to us as we identify ourselves with him in faith and obedience, for he came that we "may have life, and have it abundantly".

GOD GUARDS

"Read my favourite Psalm," said the hospital patient. "You know—the one that goes, 'I will lift up mine eyes unto the hills . . .' " So I opened the Bible and read the *121st Psalm* for the sick woman and watched the lines on her face soften as she realized that what was once true for a Hebrew poet was also true for her. This Psalm has proved a source of strength for many people, especially in times of personal crisis. The opening words, *"I will lift up mine eyes . . ."* suggest the posture and mood of prayer—man, the creature, looking in his need to his Creator God. Someone has said that in crisis we look inwards and become afraid, we look around us and become confused, we look upwards and become serene.

This is one of the Pilgrimage Psalms. Every devout Jew at least once in his lifetime made a pilgrimage to Jerusalem. I sensed this ecstasy when I first made that pilgrimage a number of years ago. As the pinnacles of the Holy City came into view, I echoed the song of praise, "I was glad when they said unto me, Let us go into the house of the Lord. Our feet shall stand within thy gates, O Jerusalem." The ancient Jew did not go by himself to the great festivals. He would join a caravan that flowed like a tributary into the river of pilgrims moving towards the Holy City. At the age of twelve the boy Jesus went with his parents, and so large was the company that on the homeward journey Mary and Joseph had travelled for a whole day before noticing that their son was not with the other children. These pilgrimages could be dangerous. Always the pilgrims had to be on guard against the perils of the journey—exposure, thirst, hunger, illness, accident, sudden attack by lurking brigands. Like soldiers on a route march they sang to keep up their morale. At night they posted sentries on the surrounding hills and again, sitting by their campfires, they sang songs of assurance like that which has been preserved in the 121st Psalm.

"I will lift up mine eyes unto the hills . . ." The older version

of the Bible adds, *"from whence cometh my help,"* suggesting that the pilgrims found a source of security in the hills themselves. Later versions come nearer to the mind of the Psalmist when they punctuate his words differently and rephrase them in the form of a question. "I will lift up mine eyes unto the hills". (Full stop.) "From whence cometh my help?" (Question mark). And he answers his question—*"My help cometh from the Lord, which made heaven and earth."* Not the hills themselves but the Creator of those hills, not the figure of the sentry outlined against the night sky but the Eternal Sentry whom that figure represents—*he* is the source of security; it is he who watches over his people and guards them against danger.

We have long since taken this familiar Psalm from its original, historical setting. The picture of God watching over the Jewish pilgrims on their way to Jerusalem has become a picture of the God who watches over all of us on our pilgrimage through time to the eternal city in heaven. He is *a God who guards*, who might indeed be called our Divine Bodyguard. An important man, like a king or president, is always accompanied by strong, burly, wide-awake characters who are responsible for his personal safety. They are never far away from him, they may even sleep outside his door, they try to stand between him and all danger. We call them his bodyguards. The 121st Psalm pictures God standing in this relationship to every man who believes in him and trusts him. He is our Bodyguard through life's pilgrimage, and the Psalm shows how faithfully he fulfils that role.

He is a God who stays close to us at every step of the journey. This is suggested in the words, *"He will not suffer thy foot to be moved,"* better translated, "He will not let thy foot slip". Our God does not simply guard us from a distance, like a police force to be telephoned in time of dire calamity. His protection is more immediate and personal. He stands nearby at all times, ready to reach out his arm and steady us lest we make the slightest slip.

One of the great truths about God, which has been redis-covered by modern theology, is the truth that he is a God beside us. For too long we have thought of him only as a God "up there" or "out there", a remote and distant Deity who dwells somewhere in outer space beyond the farthest galaxy. No need to kill off this transcendent god, else we cease to worship him as God and we ignore a large part of the Bible. God is still "the high and lofty One that inhabiteth eternity," who "sits above the circle of the earth, and its inhabitants are like grasshoppers". But the Bible teaches that he who "telleth the number of the stars" is also he who "healeth the broken in heart, and bindeth up their wounds". The God beyond us is also a God beside us. Paul reminded the philosophers in Athens that this transcendent God "is not far from each one of us, for in him we live and move and have our being".

The Psalmist gave voice to this faith when he declared that God is so near that "he will not suffer thy foot to be moved". Presumably he wrote out of his own experience. He could say, as many a man can say, that he had reached out his hand and touched the hand of God. How can we Christians ever doubt God's nearness if we believe that he really did break through eternity into time and clothe himself in the flesh of Jesus Christ? It is the truth of the Incarnation, and especially of the beautiful stories of our Lord's lowly birth and childhood, that God has entered all the way into our human experience. Once and for all he came where we are and identified himself with us, made our life his life, our peril his peril, our suffering his suffering. Through the presence and power of his living Holy Spirit God remains within our experience, a God close beside us on life's journey, a Divine Bodyguard who "will not suffer thy foot to be moved."

This Divine Bodyguard, of whom the Psalmist sings, *never rests, never leaves his post, never goes off duty*. Night falls on the pilgrims' camp. The weary travellers, with one last look at the sentries on the hills, can fall asleep confidently knowing that these faithful guardians will keep watch through the night. But what if weariness overcomes the sentries, and they also fall asleep? Who will warn the pilgrims of approaching danger, and who will defend them and their children against wild animals and murderous robbers? In this fear the pilgrim lifts up his eyes and looks above the hills, beyond the human sentries, past all earthly securities, and commits himself in prayer to the God who never grows weary, the unsleeping God who watches over him and protects him day and night. This God is the Great Insomniac. "*He that keepeth thee will not slumber. Behold, he that keepeth Israel shall neither slumber nor sleep.*"

K

There was a Methodist Bishop, Dr. Quayle, who wrote some helpful books for the guidance of young ministers. He tells that once, when he was burning the midnight oil, he happened to glance at the open Bible on his desk, and his eyes fell on these words in the 121st Psalm, "He that keepeth thee will not slumber". It seemed like the voice of God saying to him, "There's no need for both of us to stay up all night, Quayle. I'm going to stay up anyway. You go to bed and get a good sleep." What keeps people awake, turning and tossing on their beds, their mental machinery running at full blast, so that they are denied the sleep essential to their daily renewal of strength? Noise, perhaps, or fear. The child may be afraid of the dark and of sinking into helpless unconsciousness; it is a fear that many people never outgrow. In middle-age it may be the fear of letting go, the refusal to relinquish the responsibilities and problems which we faced today and will have to face again tomorrow. Have we the faith to commit our concerns to God, even for the space of a single night, believing that the God who has guarded us during our waking hours will guard us while we sleep and, not only so, but will stay awake working actively on our behalf, strengthening us for the next day's responsibilities and perhaps even solving some of our problems? That was the Psalmist's experience of God. "He that keepeth thee will not slumber."

God guards us against all the dangers of the journey. "*The Lord is thy keeper: the Lord is thy shade upon thy right hand.*" The Psalm specifies two dangers which were more than figures of speech in their original setting: "*The sun shall not smite thee by day, nor the moon by night.*" These were, in fact, the two perils that the pilgrims dreaded most. Sunstroke was an ever-present danger, as anyone who has travelled through desert countries knows. Men can go blind and mad, they can die of thirst by prolonged exposure to the sun's scorching rays. There was a lot of superstition bound up in the fear of moon-stroke, but you realize its reality when you remember that the word "lunacy" comes from it. The Psalmist could not have offered more suggestive figures of speech to describe how completely God guards us against all the perils of the day and the night. There are many dangers in life's pilgrimage. We shall not escape them but neither shall we allow them to terrify us, because we know that we are not unprotected. We have a Bodyguard, a Keeper, one who is our shade upon our right hand.

In 1915, when Ernest Shackleton tried to cross the Antarctic, his ship was crushed in the ice, and his whole party stranded in three small boats. Leaving most of his men at Elephant Island, Shackleton and two companions started across a thousand miles of terrifying sea and through some of the worst weather in the world. They reached the Island of S. Georgia, but on the wrong side, so they had to cross an unexplored mountain range, over six thousand feet high. These were not mountaineers but seamen, yet they reached the crest of a pass at the end of the day. Here they were trapped, for they could not cut steps down the sheer side of the cliff. "We'll slide," said Shackleton, and the three of them sat on their coils of rope, held fast to one another and took off in the darkness. Miraculously they arrived at the bottom safely. Shackleton's typical British comment was, "It's not good to do that kind of thing too often." Writing about this experience, he said that he had the strange feeling that there were not three men but four on the perilous trek. He said nothing to the other two, but one of them remarked to him, "Boss, I had a curious feeling on the march that there was another person with us." The third man said that he had felt the same way.

This is not fantasy but one of the great truths about God in our human experience. "The Lord is thy keeper: the Lord is thy shade upon thy right hand." It was the Psalmist's experience of God and it may have been yours—the sense of an unseen Presence at your side bringing you safely through the perils that should have destroyed you. There was that time in your childhood when you found your way home after being lost in a dense forest; there was that day in your youth when you nearly drowned. In later life you made an astonishing recovery from a serious illness, or you cleared a level-crossing a split second ahead of the train, or you miraculously escaped a bombing raid. At the time you laughingly referred to your "guardian angel" but deep down you gave thanks to a protecting Providence.

God guards us in the way that really matters. There are times when bodyguards seem helpless, as they were helpless to protect

President Kennedy against the assassin's bullet. There must have been times when the ancient pilgrims, trusting God to shield them against the sun and the moon and other perils of the journey, did in fact come into contact with these perils and perish beneath them. Would the pilgrim still sing, "The Lord is thy keeper," after robbers had devastated his camp and abducted his women and left him to die in the wilderness? Yes, he would still sing it, though perhaps in a minor key and with this variation, *The Lord shall preserve thee from all evil; he shall preserve thy soul.*"

There is a touching incident in the life of St. Giles, patron saint of Edinburgh. Travelling through the land preaching the Gospel, he had as his constant companion a deer which he greatly loved. When they came to a village, he would point to the deer in his sermons and quote the Psalmist, "As the deer panteth after the waterbrooks, so panteth my soul after thee, O God." One day, as Giles and his dumb friend were passing through a forest, they heard dogs barking. Frightened, the deer started to run, with its master in hot pursuit. Suddenly Giles saw a huntsman fitting an arrow to his bow, ready to shoot the fleeting animal. Instinctively Giles stretched out his arm in the direction of his pet. He was just in the line of the arrow's flight. It pierced his hand and struck the deer in the side, but Giles' hand had so broken the arrow's force that it wounded the animal only superficially.

It is a figure of God in our human experience. As our unseen Bodyguard he may not always shield our flesh against the arrow of misfortune but he always breaks the force of misfortune and prevents the arrow from penetrating our vital organs and wounding us mortally. God guards us in the way that really matters—not against suffering, perhaps, but against the evils that suffering brings, the evil of bitterness and cynicism and murmuring and complaining and despair. God guards the soul, the personality, the inner citadel of the self which is the seat of human happiness and misery. Jesus said, "Do not fear those who kill the body but cannot kill the soul"; and he had a right to say it because on Calvary's Cross he was the hand of God coming between us and every power of evil, taking in his flesh the full force of the arrow's flight so that, though it strikes us, it need not wound us more than superficially.

The concluding verse of this beloved Psalm promises that our Divine Bodyguard on life's pilgrimage *will see us through to the end of the journey.* *"The Lord shall preserve thy going out and thy coming in from this time forth, and even for evermore."* It was very fitting that the hospital patient, to whom I referred at the outset, should ask me to read the 121st Psalm, because the next morning she was to undergo surgery. I asked her to repeat the last verse and to keep repeating it before the operation. I said, "The Lord shall preserve thy going out . . . he will be watching over you when the anaesthetic drugs your consciousness; and thy coming in . . . he will be watching over you when you regain consciousness in the recovery room. Through all this ordeal of suffering the Divine Bodyguard will not leave your side. He will see you through."

Surely the Psalmist's affirmation of faith has a more ultimate meaning for all of us. Surely we can take his words upon our lips and keep repeating them when we come to the last great crisis. If we are Christians, if we believe that Jesus Christ died and rose from the dead, we shall know that death is a sleeping and an awakening, a going out and a coming in. And we shall not be afraid of this last great crisis if we can believe that God is with us and will see us through.

It is told of Abraham Lincoln that, visiting a military hospital, he stopped at the bedside of a dying soldier. The lad did not recognize his President. "Is there anything I can do for you?" asked Lincoln. "Yes," replied the boy, "I should be grateful if you would write to my mother." So, as the dying soldier painfully dictated his letter, Lincoln wrote it down. Then the lad said, "Now will you sign it so that my mother will know that you were so kind." Lincoln signed his name, and when the soldier saw the signature, an expression of awe came into his face. "I didn't know that I was bothering the President," he said. Lincoln spoke tenderly, "Is there anything else I can do?" The dying lad hesitated a moment, then said, "Would it be asking too much, sir? It won't be long now. It would be easier to die if you would stay and see me through." So Lincoln sat by the bed. Eleven o'clock came, twelve, one, two, three; and then, just as the first faint streaks of dawn were appearing in the sky, the spirit of the young soldier took its silent flight. The President gently closed the sightless eyes, folded the hands on the soldier's breast and with bowed head went out of the ward. He had kept his word. He had stayed at the boy's side. He had seen him through.

Once more it is a figure of God in man's experience, the kind of God with whom we have to do—a Divine Bodyguard on life's pilgrimage who stays close beside us and never sleeps, who guards us against every danger and guards us in the way that really matters. This God has given us his word that he will see us through to the end of the journey. He will be with us when night falls and we go into the darkness; he will be there to meet us when morning breaks and the shadows flee away. "The Lord shall preserve thy going out and thy coming in from this time forth, and even for evermore."

GOD INTERVENES

There was a director of a camp for underprivileged boys who very seldom broke up a fist-fight. He might punish the assailants afterwards but he usually allowed them to fight it out. He hated bullying and tried to teach his lads the rules of fair play but, if two campers did come to blows, he rarely interfered. He believed that every boy must learn to fight his own battles and not look for help when he was getting the worst of it. Once in a while this wise camp director made an exception. On one occasion a group of bullies began terrorizing the whole camp. During the day they would send word to some smaller lad that they intended coming to his tent that night to beat him up and they gloated at the thought of his fearful reaction. One little fellow, after getting the grim warning, trembled in terror half the night but he might as well have gone to sleep, because his attackers never arrived. In fact, he never saw them again. When the camp director heard of this juvenile "protection-racket" he stepped in promptly and sent the offenders home.

Is that a true picture of God in man's experience? Can we think of him as a Divine Camp Director, watching over his unruly brood, who steps in and takes sides when the strong rise up to exploit the weak? We are at once repelled and attracted by the idea. The thought of God taking sides conjures up all the wars in history when men have prayed for the annihilation of their enemies because they believed that God was fighting on their side. It recalls a modern play in which a middle-class business-man surveys his prosperity and piously declares, "I have never doubted that God was on my side." This seems a crude theology, and we pride ourselves on having outgrown it. We consider it more enlightened and mature to think of God not as an external factor who brings us help from outside our situation but as an internal factor always at work within our situation. We are about ready to dispense with the idea of a God who takes sides.

Yet that would be a pity, because it means that we miss one

of the great truths of the Bible—not an academic truth, either, but a fact of human experience. The *124th Psalm* closes with a verse often used by Christian congregations as a Call to Worship: "*Our help is in the name of the Lord, who made heaven and earth.*" Like many Old Testament verses it takes on larger meaning when we lift it from context and place it under the magnifying-glass of the New Testament; and like many Bible verses it becomes more meaningful when we read the verses that lead up to it:

"*If it had not been the Lord who was on our side, now may Israel say;*

If it had not been the Lord who was on our side, when men rose up against us;

Then they had swallowed us up quick, when their wrath was kindled against us:

Then the waters had overwhelmed us, the stream had gone over our soul:

Then the proud waters had gone over our soul.

Blessed be the Lord, who hath not given us as a prey to their teeth.

Our soul is escaped as a bird out of the snare of the fowlers: the snare is broken, and we are escaped.

Our help is in the name of the Lord, who made heaven and earth."

This is another of the Pilgrimage Psalms which the ancient Jews used to sing like marching-songs on their way to the great festivals at Jerusalem. They sang to keep up their morale, because these journeys could be exhausting and dangerous. The travellers passed through wild, mountainous country which was a happy-hunting-ground for bandits and brigands and, when they camped for the night, they were like sitting ducks that could be wiped out by a single surprise attack. The 124th Psalm suggests that there must have been at least one occasion when such a disaster nearly happened to a company of pilgrims. Suddenly "men rose up against them"; and so fierce were these enemies that the Psalmist compares them to a primeval monster that swallows up its victims, to raging floodwaters that create chaos, to a trap that snares a helpless animal. The end had surely come. There could be no escape for the helpless pilgrims. Yet the amazing thing is that they did escape, they passed through the danger unscathed. It was as though a miracle had happened, as though an invisible hand had interposed to drive off the monster, push back the floodwaters and release the deadly trap. Where did this unexpected help come from? The Psalmist answers with complete confidence: "Our help is in the name of the Lord, who made heaven and earth."

The picture of God that emerges from the 124th Psalm is the picture of *a God who intervenes,* a God who takes sides with the weak when the strong rise up to destroy them. It is a picture drawn from human experience and it does not stand alone, because the whole record of God's dealings with his people in the Old Testament shows him consistently to be that kind of God. Again and again he intervenes at the eleventh hour to save his people from certain disaster. Out of Egypt come a million slaves, pursued by the armies of Pharoah, their escape cut off by the forbidding waters of the Red Sea. They are trapped. Suddenly and unexpectedly a strong east wind drives back the shallow waters and drops after the Israelites have crossed in safety. On the heights of Mount Tabor a tiny Hebrew garrison looks helplessly at Sisera's great attacking army in the valley below. What chance have they against those gleaming chariots? Suddenly clouds fill the sky, and a torrential rain turns the valley into a bog, immobilizing the chariots, demoralizing the invader and giving Israel such a victory that it could be said, "The stars in their courses fought against Sisera." Within the walls of Jerusalem the terrified citizens await the crushing blow from Sennacherib, the Assyrian dictator, who boasts that he has them shut up like a bird in a cage. The blow never falls. At dawn they see no sign of the besieging army and, when they venture near the Assyrian camp, they find it wiped out by a sudden deadly disease. This is the activity of God in the Old Testament, a God who takes sides with the weak and intervenes when the strong rise up to destroy them.

The Bible sees no conflict between the idea of an immanent God who works within our human situation and the idea of a transcendent God who intervenes from outside. That conflict has been created by modern theology. The Bible sees God as both immanent and transcendent. The God beside and within us is also the God above and beyond us, the high and lofty One that inhabiteth eternity, the Creator and Controller of the universe. Because God is sovereign, because he rules the world which he created, he does preserve the right and the power to intervene in its affairs and to shape them according to his purposes and preferences. We can truthfully share the conviction of the Psalmist who said, "Our help is in the name of the Lord, who made heaven and earth."

Exaggerated publicity has been given to a trio of theologians in the United States who have announced without any sorrow that "God is dead". They proclaim the demise not of some little, inadequate, man-made image of God but of God himself. God, they tell us, has actually died; and we wonder what process of logic led them to this seemingly blasphemous conclusion. One of them, Thomas J. J. Altizer, proposes the novel theory that God died on the Cross, All that God was—was in Christ. And Christ died on the Cross—therefore God died on the Cross in order to let man assume his responsibilities in the world.

We can only say that the writers of the New Testament would be utterly astonished by this amazing logic, because they also believed that God was in Christ and that Christ died on the Cross but they did not believe that the Cross meant the death of all that there was of God. The very opposite, in fact. They believed that, though Jesus was dead, God was very much alive and that he showed himself to be a living, powerful and active God when he raised Jesus from the dead. They saw the Resurrection of Christ as God's mightiest intervention in the affairs of men, the supreme evidence that he is a God who takes sides with the weak when the strong rise up to destroy them. Men rose up against Jesus, giving grim reality to all those figures of speech coined by the Psalmist to describe the peril of the pilgrims. The monster of Roman power swallowed Jesus, the raging floodwaters of religious hypocrisy threw his brief ministry into chaos, a rock-hewn tomb held his lifeless body in a trap. God was in Christ, but Christ was crucified, dead and buried. He was finished. Then a miracle happened. An invisible hand interposed to drive off the monster, push back the floodwaters and release the deadly trap. Where did this unexpected help come from? The New Testament writers would echo the Psalmist with complete confidence: "Our help is in the name of the Lord, who made heaven and earth."

A few years ago, when some *avant-garde* theologians began

telling us that the Resurrection stories are not history but symbolic myths, a former Bishop of London told of an argument between two scholars. One of them said, "The Empty Tomb does not matter." The other replied, "Remove the Empty Tomb from Christianity, and we have nothing left." Certainly we have nothing left of the New Testament. It may be argued that we should still have a large proportion of the Gospels with their marvellous pictures of the Man Jesus, their record of his ministry, their account of his teachings and their description of his sacrificial death, but it needs to be remembered that the Gospels would never have been written if the men who wrote them had not believed that God raised Jesus from the dead. The four books known as "Gospels" are among the later writings of the New Testament. The earliest writings, i.e. the written records of the earliest Christian sermons, can be found in the opening chapters of the *Acts of the Apostles* and they take their starting-point not with the birth of Jesus or his life, ministry, teachings and death but with the historical fact that God raised him from the dead. The Resurrection is not an epilogue to the story of Christ; it is the basis, the essence, the impulse of that story, the inspiration of the New Testament and the constitutive truth of our Christian Faith.

Let us repeat that truth loudly and clearly. At Easter the Church does not celebrate a resuscitated corpse—after all, medical science can perform that miracle—it celebrates the mightiest act of God's intervention in history. The Empty Tomb matters because it demonstrates that the God with whom we have to do is an active, powerful, sovereign God who not only lived and worked in Jesus but who worked outside Jesus to raise him from the dead. We can trust this God, we can count on him, we can heed the *Epistle of Peter* which declares about Jesus, "Through him you have confidence in God, who raised him from the dead and gave him glory, so that your faith and hope are in God". This is indeed the God of the Old Testament Psalmist, the God who intervenes, who sides with the weak when the strong rise up to destroy them. Knowing this God, we can sing with the Psalmist, "Our help is in the name of the Lord, who made heaven and earth."

The Church needs to sing that song with new conviction, because these are days when the Church in many parts of the world seems to be fighting for its existence. The situation is not new. Down the centuries the Church has often been like a pilgrim people, travelling through dangerous country and threatened by crafty enemies. Time and again men have risen up against the Church, and their enmity has been fierce like that of a primeval monster that swallows up its victims, like raging floodwaters that create chaos, like a trap that snares a helpless animal. Time and again the Church has seemed doomed to extinction, yet the amazing thing is that always a miracle has happened, as though an invisible hand interposed to drive off the monster, push back the floodwaters and release the deadly trap. Where did this unexpected help come from? The Church has answered with complete confidence, "Our help is in the name of the Lord, who made heaven and earth."

How else shall we explain the Church's survival through the early centuries? Its original adherents were peasants and slaves without any advantages of wealth or learning or political power, the weakest classes in Roman society. Evil men rose up against them, dubbed them atheists, derided them as haters of the human race and falsely charged them with perpetrating the grossest immoralities. One Roman Emperor ordered some of them wrapped in the hides of wild beasts and torn to pieces by dogs; others he fastened to crosses and set on fire to illuminate a circus staged for the crowds in his own gardens. Persistently and viciously persecuted, early Christianity seemed doomed, yet within a few hundred years one could read this paragraph in a letter written by a Christian Bishop:

"Even in Rome itself paganism is left in solitude. The Egyptian Serapis has become a Christian. The Huns have learned the Psalter. The chilly Cynthians are warmed by the faith. Every pagan temple in Rome is covered with cobwebs. They who once were the gods of the nation remain under their leaking, lonely roofs with horned owls and other birds of the night."

In Communist Russia men have risen up against the Church and reduced it, so they think, to a remnant of peasants, anticipating that Christianity will eventually die with them. Should you doubt that fact, read the distinguished book by Michael Bourdeaux entitled *Opium of the People*[1] which is an authentic

[1] Faber and Faber, London, 1965.

and carefully-documented survey of the present state of the
Christian religion in Russia. Mr. Bourdeaux, who speaks
Russian fluently and has spent several periods in that country,
including a year of graduate study at Moscow University, describes the ridicule heaped on Christian pupils in the classrooms
of state schools and the brutal persecution of theological
students by members of the Komsomol (the young Communist
League to which all secular students are virtually forced to
belong). He also describes the amazing vitality of some of the
Russian churches, the stubborn survival of the Faith in older
people who have lived through the long years of persecution,
the still more astounding conversions to Christianity among
students who have measured it against Communism and felt
its claim upon their lives. Looking at the Church in areas of
persecution today, one thinks of the man in *Pilgrim's Progress*
who pours water on a fire burning against a wall but cannot
extinguish it because behind the wall, hidden from view,
another man continually pours oil on the fire so that it burns
higher and hotter.

John Calvin spoke the truth when he said that the story of
the Church is a story of many resurrections. The miracle of
Easter did not occur only once. That miracle has recurred
constantly in the life of the Church, distinguishing it from all
other societies of men. It is a fact of the Church's history that,
when everything in its own life and in the life of the world
points to its approaching death, a strange power of inward
renewal begins to operate that releases the forces of life and
hope. The awareness of this truth should be the great factor
saving us from all the current cynicism about the Church's
future. Beyond any doubt, the Church does have powerful
enemies in the secular culture, men who rise up to crucify it;
and it may well be that there is much in the life of the Church
that ought to be crucified. The Church as we know it may
become a corpse, but God can resurrect a corpse. He can bring
the dead back to life; and we have hope that he will do this for
the Church, because he has shown himself in man's experience
to be a god who intervenes.

We must not miss the importance of this truth for our
personal lives. Perhaps we can see ourselves in the 124th
Psalm because we are all pilgrims making our journey through

time to the Heavenly Jerusalem in eternity. It can be a hazard-
ous journey, fraught with perils which, though not always
embodied in human flesh, do rise up against us and threaten
to destroy us. How aptly those same figures of speech describe
the dangers that beset our earthly pilgrimage! The woman
whose husband is a problem drinker can speak of his uncontrollable habit as a primeval monster that may one day swallow
up their home. The personal tragedies that some people
suffer—the breakdowns in health, the loss of loved ones, the
reverses in business—are like raging floodwaters that throw
their little lives into chaos. The burdens we have to bear, the
exhausting duties from which there is no escape, the circle of
monotonous routine that we travel day by day, can seem like
a trap which snares a helpless animal. Even now *you* may feel
so weak and so overpowered by the forces that rise up against
you that you look at the helpless pilgrims in the 124th Psalm
and say with feeling, "That's me! I'm beaten, doomed, finished!
My situation is hopeless!"

But is any situation altogether hopeless? I once read an
inspiring novel by Thomas Savage called *A Bargain with God.*
It told the story of an Anglican priest who knew and loved all
the people in his parish, especially Johnny and Jebby Moss
whom he had married and whose baby he had baptized. One
day a fire gutted the building where the Moss family lived,
taking the life of their little daughter. Johnny bore the tragedy
bravely, but Jebby was numb with grief. She withdrew into
herself, refused to speak to anybody, scarcely recognized her
husband and simply sang songs all day to the doll which had
belonged to their child. Desperate to see his wife herself again,
Johnny went to Father Ferris and poured out his anguish.
What could he do? Father Ferris said, "Johnny, there's only
one thing you can do. Sometimes things are too much for us
alone. You and Jebby must put the past behind you . . . and
that is very hard. Ask for help, Johnny." The faint hope in
Johnny's eyes vanished. He said dully, "You mean pray?"
Father Ferris replied, "Prayers are answered. Not just the
prayers for strength and courage, but the others too." Johnny
said, "I never thought much about miracles." The priest
answered him gently, "It is hard to believe, but if the greatest
miracle happened, of course the little ones can, and we know
that the great one happened." Johnny was puzzled. "What

do you mean?" he asked. "I mean," said Father Ferris, "that Jesus Christ rose from the dead."

It comes down to that. If God raised Jesus from the dead, if he had once and for all shown himself, as he showed himself in the experience of a Hebrew Psalmist, to be a God who intervenes and takes sides with the weak when the strong rise up to destroy them, then it means that he is a God to whom we can pray and from whom we can expect what may appear to us as miracles. It means that no situation is ever hopeless, because even in the darkest hour that we can ever imagine our help will be "in the name of the Lord, who made heaven and earth."

GOD CALMS

In this age of computers and labour-saving devices, which afford us more and more leisure time, do you not think it strange that so many people are living on the edge of a nervous breakdown? Modern man moves at a hectic pace; he lives at a feverish pitch. His nerves are in a constant state of stress and tension, and he can find no rest, no peace. He tries to soothe his excited nerves with alcohol, sleeping drugs, tranquillizer pills, physiotherapy and weekends in the country—anything to stop his hands from trembling, anything to help him relax. Some of us know from first-hand experience that the great problem of our lives these days is how to achieve a sense of inner calm.

The experience of a Hebrew Psalmist comes close to our need. One Old Testament scholar called the writer of the *131st Psalm* a "hot-blooded man". He seems to have been an excited man, perhaps the ancient type of the modern go-getter who with unusual conceit reaches for the stars. Like his modern counterpart he had travelled every day from morning till night in high gear, his pride, envy and pretentiousness giving him no rest, no peace. But something had happened to him, something that changed the whole picture and altered his mood completely. Like a squalling baby, soothed at his mother's breast, he had ceased his convulsive crying and found a deep sense of inner contentment and calm.

What had, in fact, happened to the Psalmist? His words tell their own story: "*I do not occupy myself with things too great and too marvellous for me. But I have calmed and quieted my soul,*"[1] Somewhere in a moment of clear insight this man had come to terms with himself. He had proclaimed an armistice in the civil war between his ambitions and his limitations. He had resigned from the rat race. He had decided to stop reaching for the stars. It took courage to make that decision and even greater courage to confess it openly, but the effect seems to

[1] This chapter follows the text of the Revised Standard Version.

have been a spiritual rebirth like starting life all over again. The "big shot" turned "little shot" has to swallow a lot of his pride, but it probably makes the most nutritious meal he has ever eaten. It can be humiliating to step down and settle for something less than the stars, but it's better to go through life with a humbled heart than with a heart that pounds until it bursts.

This is not an easy decision to make, especially in a competitive society that worships the cult of success. How did the Psalmist do it? Simply give up the struggle because of the fatigue and disillusionment of middle-age? Simply quit trying like a distance runner who slows down to a walk because he knows that he cannot win anyway? The 131st Psalm may be brief, only three verses in all, but as a spiritual autobiography it leaves nothing to the imagination. "*Hope in the Lord,*" writes the Psalmist. This man had brought God into his experience and, in doing so, discovered a great truth—that there is really no wealth in life, no knowledge, no success, nothing that gives a man a deep and lasting sense of fulfilment unless it comes as a gift from God. The awakening to this truth can have a profoundly calming effect on a man's soul. Not that he becomes a defeatist. He still gives his utmost, still encounters life, but not with a chip on his shoulder any more, not with a "By heaven, I'll beat this racket!" attitude. Instead, with full recognition of his own limitations and undergirded by his faith, a man does the best he can and leaves the issue to God. He discovers, as the Psalmist discovered, that our God is *a God who calms.*

We can see at least four possibilities for the writer of the 131st Psalm. He may have been a *careerist*, ambitious in a worldly, materialistic sense. If he were alive today he would be the sort who wants to get ahead and make the most of his opportunities and climb to the top of the ladder professionally and socially. Perhaps he was, in fact, a merchant or a landowner, blessed with a natural ambition to work hard and make money and generally succeed.

There is nothing vulgar about that. Society owes its progress to men and women who rise above the level of mediocrity and pursue their careers, driven by the honest ambition to succeed. We should still be writing letters with quill pens,

L

still travelling by horse and buggy, still dying of diphtheria, unless someone at some time had been ambitious enough to invent typewriters, jet aeroplanes and vaccine. Yet we must reckon with the danger that a man's ambition can be a destroying passion; it can run away with him and make him a nervous wreck. There was a novel popular a few years ago called *The Man in the Gray Flannel Suit*. It told the story of Tom, a typical young salesman, goaded on by his employer, pressured by competition, consumed by his own lust for money and power, who drove himself like a machine, senseless of what success was costing him. One day, before it was too late, he took stock of himself, faced the fact that he had been reaching for the stars and decided that, if he wanted to recover his sanity and hold his home together, he would have to revise his goals and be satisfied with something less than the stars.

Many of us, if we want to recover our poise, will have to face that truth eventually. While we owe it to ourselves to achieve our highest potential, we shall not make a success of life—the whole of life, not just our daily work which is only one department of life—until we proclaim an armistice in the civil war between our ambitions and our limitations. Somewhere along the way we have to submit to the humbling discipline of honest self-assessment. We have to decide that the Creator has given us just so much energy and just so much ability and, inspired by these realities, not by some grandiose vision, make our contribution to the common good.

In that decision the Hebrew poet found a deep sense of inner contentment and calm. Yet it was more than a human decision, more than a realistic coming to terms with his own limitations. This man achieved peace of mind by bringing into his experience a whole new dimension—the fulfilment of God's purpose for his life. "Hope in the Lord," he writes; and at this point his words have an imperative mood that speaks to us in our tension and stress. When we do place our hope in the Lord, rather than in our own animal heat and activity, we may be surprised to discover that God has more ambitious plans for us that we have for ourselves. We discover also that the fulfilment of these plans depends less upon the measure in which we work than upon the measure in which God works in and through us. We achieve the serenity of surrender. We acknowledge that the enterprise of our life belongs to God and we try to obey him, trusting his promise that his grace will supply all our need.

It is possible also that the writer of the 131st Psalm was *a theologian*, deeply engaged in the study of the science of God and searching for the truth about ultimate things. Here again he teaches us the importance of coming to terms with our limitations.

His opening words, "*O Lord, my heart is not lifted up, my eyes are not raised too high*," find an echo in the New Testament. You hear it in a parable of Jesus—"And the publican, standing afar off, would not lift up so much as his eyes unto heaven". It is a posture of humility, an acknowledgement of the infinite distance between man and God, a confession that the Being of God is a Being clothed in mystery; and you don't tie mystery up in neat bundles of understanding. Must we understand a mystery, however, in order to appropriate it? A small boy asked an old sailor, "What is the wind?" After a long pause the sailor answered, "I don't know. I can't tell you. But I know how to hoist a sail". Endless questions about the winds of God baffle even the most profound theologians. You will go spiritually berserk trying to answer them all. But the wind of God is real. Believe in it, hoist your sail to it and you may find serenity and peace.

"I do not occupy myself with things too great and marvellous for me. But I have calmed and quieted my soul." No spiritual defeatism in these words; they are a sublime expression of faith. Let us suppose that the Psalmist has, in fact, been a seeker for truth, reaching up to heaven and by instinct and philosophy striving to solve the mystery of Ultimate Being. He still seeks the truth about God, but not aggressively any more; instead receptively, knowing that what God is and what it is to be Divine is something that a man can learn only where God reveals it to him. Again we can hear an echo in the New Testament. It comes from Jesus, comforting his disciples in the Upper Room: "I have yet many things to say to you, but you cannot bear them now. When the Spirit of truth comes, he will guide you into all the truth." Ultimate truth is of God, and God's Spirit leads us into it in his own way and his own time as we are able to grasp and digest it. To understand Divine Truth we need *not* the sophisticated minds of philosophers but the receptive minds of little children; these alone have eyes to see God.

Supremely the 131st Psalm is an expression of obedience. Read it aloud:

> "*O Lord, my heart is not lifted up,*
>   *my eyes are not raised too high;*
> *I do not occupy myself with things too great*
>   *and too marvellous for me.*
> *But I have calmed and quieted my soul,*
>   *like a child quieted at its mother's breast;*
>   *like a child that is quieted is my soul.*
> *O Israel, hope in the Lord*
>   *from this time forth and for evermore.*"

These words have melody, a haunting theme that recurs constantly in the Bible. You hear it unmistakably in the Garden of Gethsemane where Jesus wrestles with the will of God and, finding that will too great and marvellous even for his understanding, calms and quiets his soul in lowly obedience. "My Father, if this cannot pass unless I drink it, thy will be done." The heart of the Christian life is not intellectual understanding, not mysticism, not piety, but obedience. The Psalmist comes close to our needs when he says, in effect, "Hush your anxious questionings. Settle for something less than the stars, something less than perfect understanding of the will of God. Obey God's will in the measure that he has revealed it to you and leave the issue to him."

The Hebrew poet may have been *a moral and social idealist*. That would have been in keeping with his character. Many of Israel's Prophets and Psalmists felt themselves Divinely called to denounce national evils and elevate the moral tone of Jewish society. In this respect our Psalmist may have occupied himself with great and marvellous things and in this respect he may have been forced to come to terms with his own limitations. Perhaps he faced the truth that many an idealist needs to face—that reaching for the stars can be a noble form of escapism, a concern with the impossible as an excuse for evading the possible.

So, perhaps the Psalmist took stock of his own situation. Perhaps he analyzed it realistically. He could not eradicate social corruption, but what could he do? He could try to conduct his own affairs with integrity. He could not expurgate the nation's lust but he could keep his own heart pure. He could not eliminate juvenile delinquency but he could discipline his own children. He could not put an end to wars but he could make peace in his own relationships. He could not be a saint but he could be a good man. He could not clutch the stars but he could settle for something less than the stars. He could not solve the world's problems but he could try to tackle the immediate, practical problems at hand and leave the larger issues to God.

There is no suggestion here that we ought to dilute our moral and social ideals. A non-Christian psychiatrist said to a patient, "I should advise you to stop attending your church. Religion does you more harm than good; it gives you an unhealthy sense of guilt. You will never resolve your emotional difficulties until you resolve the conflict between the ideal and the actual. Stop living as you think you are supposed to live and begin living as you know that you can and want to live." But that isn't coming to terms with our moral limitations; that's letting them win the day by default, and it makes our last state worse than the first. In our society today we hear a chorus of voices, blaring at us from advertisements, television screens and popular novels, counselling us to moral mediocrity. Most of us, for the sake of our mental health, need to hear voices that counsel us to moral excellence. "You, therefore, must be perfect, as your heavenly Father is perfect"—that is not reaching for the stars; it is aiming towards the moral perfection of Christ.

Our trouble is not that we pitch our ideals too high but that we rely upon our own unaided strength of character to achieve them. We want to do what's right. We want to be better than we are and we want to build a better world, but our failure to live up to our own ideals and our failure to improve society makes us ashamed of ourselves, frustrated and disgusted. The Hebrew poet discovered that the answer to moral futility lies not in moral compromise but in religious faith. It is not what *we* achieve that matters but what God achieves through us, insofar as we yield ourselves to him in obedience and faith. "I do not occupy myself with things too great and marvellous for me"—which is another way of saying, "I don't pretend to be a saint. I do the best I can. I try to live a good life and

serve God within my own limitations. I calm and quiet my
soul in the sure faith that, however inadequate my service, God
will accept it and that what is lacking in me God will supply."

This Hebrew poet, whose words suggests that he might have
been a careerist, a theologian or an idealist, could also have
been *a sufferer*—in which case he has more to teach us about
coming to terms with our limitations. Like the unhappy Job,
he may have been hit by a personal disaster or, like the Jews in
exile whom Job represents, he may have been crushed by the
weight of national calamity. From his Psalm we infer that he
had not accepted his suffering passively but that, like Job, he
had lifted an angry face to heaven, shaken his fist at God and
demanded to know the reason why.

Most of us, when we suffer, and the pain of body or mind
becomes too intense, begin to whimper as the Psalmist did.
Excitedly we cry out, "Why did this happen to me? What have
I done to deserve it? Why doesn't God do something to stop
it?" The Psalmist admits that he whimpered, but then he tells
us that, like a child soothed at its mother's breast, he stopped
whimpering. He did so because he stopped reaching for the
stars—which means, probably, that he gave up trying to understand what mortal man can never understand. He came to
realize that some of life's experiences will never make sense to
the human mind but that, if we learn to accept them and to trust
in the wisdom and providence of God, we may at least manage
our own lives with composure.

A missionary tells of a Japanese pastor who developed the
symptoms of a throat cancer just a few weeks after his marriage
to a lovely girl. He insisted on knowing the truth about his
illness. The doctor gave him less than a year to live and advised
him to stop work and make himself as comfortable as possible.
The pastor protested, "I can't stop work now. That would
destroy the faith of my young people. I've got to show them that
my suffering and death are not evil, not meaningless. I've got to
teach them to trust in God." For more than a year, until he
could no longer speak, the dying man worked with his people,
dispelling their doubts and building up their faith by his calm
and quiet courage. Not once did he complain or rebel or demand
an explanation from God. His whole attitude was that of the
Psalmist: "I do not occupy myself with things too great and

marvellous for me. But I have calmed and quieted my soul."

It is possible that the 131st Psalm did come out of that dark period when God's people had lost their homes and their country and had been carried away to exile in a foreign land. If so, it would require a mighty exercise of faith for them to believe that, however indifferent he appeared to their sufferings, God had the situation in control and that they could trust him for the issue. It would be a daring and courageous hope that looked beyond the darkness of crucifixion and saw the resurrection of their national life and the rebirth of their homes and country. Yet that hope was all they had to hush their anxious murmuring. In that hope alone they could calm and quiet their troubled souls.

Sometimes that is all *we* have in our suffering—the faith that what we do not understand God understands, the hope that God will ultimately raise us from the darkness of death to the glorious light of rebirth. "*O Israel, hope in the Lord from this time forth and for evermore.*" Let us remember that "hope" has a richer content for us than it had for the Old Testament poet. No longer does it mean wishful thinking that everything will turn out all right. It now means certainty that the God, who had revealed his love and purpose and power in Jesus Christ, will work with us in all things for our good and will finally transform our defeats into victory. "He who did not spare his own Son but gave him up for us all, will he not also give us all things with him?" In that hope we shall come to terms with our sufferings. In that hope we shall stop "reaching for the stars". In that hope we shall not occupy ourselves with things too great and marvellous for us, but we shall calm and quiet our souls.

GOD WORKS

In his remarkable book, *Come Out The Wilderness*, Bruce Kenrick tells of a pastor who went to see an old man who lived by himself in a tenement in New York's East Harlem. The old man met him on the sidewalk, and together they made their way through the stale stench of the mouldering building to the small single room at the top that was his home. The ceiling sagged, and the dark, brown paper hung in shreds from the dirty walls. They both sat on the bed which took up three-quarters of the space. Finally the old man brought out his Bible that fell open at the Psalms, many of which he had learned by heart because he was nearly blind. His favourites were heavily thumbed, the pages were yellow and worn, and when the pastor looked at them he saw that they had one thing in common— they were all psalms of praise; not psalms of comfort for a man who lived in this grim, grey slum but psalms of thanksgiving to God.[1]

It would be impossible to use the Psalms as an aid for worship and *not* give thanks to God. Every mood known to the human heart can be found in the Hebrew Psalter, but from first to last the prevailing mood is one of thanksgiving. Someone has written, "All the way through the Book of Psalms you feel that you are walking on a smouldering volcano of praise, liable to burst out at any moment into a great flame of gratitude to God." The men who wrote the Psalms praised God endlessly, but not for material benefits—freedom, security, comfort prestige and prosperity. They had none of these things, none of the temporal blessings for which men usually give thanks to God. The Psalmists praised God for eternal blessings which are independent of time and circumstance. They praised God for himself, for what he was and for what he had done.

Chiefly the Psalmists gave thanks for what have been called the mighty works of God. They looked out on the marvellous world, they looked into their own lives, they looked back over

[1] *Op. Cit.* p. 51.

history and they saw many wonderful things which to them allowed of no explanation apart from the activity of God. They had never seen God himself but they could point to signs of his presence and power. The God of their experience was *a God who works*, a God who had done great things, and for these they gave him glory and praise.

A solo voice cannot do justice to the Hallelujah Chorus. It takes a full choir, a choir of choirs, to sing the great hymns of thanksgiving to God. To get the full impact of this mood in the Hebrew Psalter we need to listen to a choir of Psalmists chanting their praises in thrilling harmony and setting forth in a mighty chorus the greatness, the glory and the majesty of God. For its sheer simplicity, however, and because it was written for use in the temple worship, we single out *Psalm 136*, one of the less familiar songs of praise. The opening verses sound like the summons of a trumpet:

"O give thanks unto the Lord; for he is good: for his mercy endureth for ever. O give thanks unto the God of gods: for his mercy endureth for ever. O give thanks to the Lord of lords: for his mercy endureth for ever."

Having called us to worship, the Psalmist then enumerates the mighty works of God which prove him a God worthy of our worship, because he is truly God and because he has done what God alone can do.

The Psalmist calls us to praise God for his mighty work in *Creation*.

"O give thanks . . . To him alone doeth great wonders . . . To him that by wisdom made the heavens . . . that stretched out the earth above the waters . . . that made great lights . . . The sun to rule by day . . . The moon and stars to rule by night: for his mercy endureth for ever."

This Hebrew poet has obviously steeped his mind in the thought of the first chapter of *Genesis*, that wonderful poetic description of God's great scheme of creation which starts with star-dust and moves upward, step by step, to the grace and glory of human personality.

We do not have to be reminded that there are difficulties in the way of this belief. We know that the writers of the Old

Testament lived in a pre-scientific age when men explained a great many things, including Creation itself, in terms of the Supernatural. Now we are not so sure that there ever was an act of Creation. When somebody asked Bertrand Russell how he would explain the universe, he replied that the universe doesn't need an explanation. The universe is just there—that's all. His viewpoint finds support from some astronomers who look through the telescope at the farthest galaxies, millions of light years away, and pronounce their verdict that, so far as they can see, the universe never had a precise beginning, nor will it have a precise ending. There is also the fact that in many areas the role of the Supernatural has been taken over by man himself who is now beginning to perform what have always been called the mighty works of God. A modern psalmist might well chant the praises of man "who alone doeth great wonders . . . who makes great lights . . . who causes the rain to fall . . . who wipes out disease and who one day may discover in a test tube the secret of creating human life."

There is an amusing scene in the Broadway play, *Inherit the Wind*[1] which dramatizes the notorious Scopes trial in Dayton, Tennessee. It concerned a public school teacher summoned to court for questioning in his classroom the literal interpretation of the Creation story in *Genesis*. At one point in the dialogue the defending attorney, who impersonates Clarence Darrow, produces a rock which he claims to be millions of years old. His opponent, who impersonates William Jennings Bryan, protests that the rock cannot be more than six thousand years old, because Bishop Usher proved conclusively that Creation itself occurred only in the year 4004 B.C.—to be precise, on the 23rd of October in the year 4004 B.C. at 9.00 a.m. Whereupon Darrow throws the court into gales of laughter by asking sarcastically, "Was that Eastern Standard Time? It wasn't daylight-saving time, was it? Because the Lord didn't make the sun until the fourth day!"

This kind of argument is sound and correct until it confuses causes with techniques and leads to false conclusions. Clever people assume that, if they can somehow explain things scientifically, they thereby dispose of God and prove the Bible writers wrong. They ignore the fact that the writers of the Old Testa-

[1] By Jerome Lawrence and Robert E. Lee (Random House of Canada Ltd., New York and Toronto).

ment were not interested in scientific explanations. How could they be? They knew nothing about science. They wrote in poems and myths, and why not? Poetry and mythology have always enjoyed equal status with science as vehicles of the truth. The truth that laid hold on the Psalmists and which they tried to express was that the universe could not have existed eternally. It must have had a beginning and it must have had a Creator. To them the whole scheme of Creation seemed too marvellous and logical to have happened accidentally. Behind it must be a Divine Intelligence, a Creative Mind. It must be the mighty work of God.

There are two ways of looking at the fact that man himself is now able to perform some of the works of God. We can see him taking God's place or we can see him growing up and becoming the man that God created him to be. The fact that we are learning to use the environment in which God placed us does not rule out the possibility that God created that environment in the first place. Someone has said that, though the Ford family owns the Ford Motor Company, yet if Mr. Ford set out by himself to build one Model-T, he would soon discover his dependence on natural resources all over the earth and within the earth which he did not create and which he cannot create. Man probes the secrets of nature, but they are still the secrets of nature. He manipulates the scheme of things but he does not add anything to the scheme of things. He makes new combinations and arrangements but he does it all within the order of God's creation. Man works the works of God, but they are still the works of God.

In that sense the Psalmists of the Old Testament call us to praise God for his mighty work in Creation. Their spirit was caught up by a scientist, an American university president, who once offered this childlike, yet profoundly reverent prayer at a convocation: "O Lord, we thank thee for the oxygen gas; we thank thee for the hydrogen gas; and for all the gases. We thank thee for the cerebrum; we thank thee for the cerebellum, and for the medulla oblongata. Amen." Such a prayer might be surprising if it came from a university sophomore, but not coming from a university president, because the president is usually the humbler of the two. Many great scientists, looking directly into the world of Nature—Robert Boyle called it "God's other Bible"—have felt a sense of awe and a mood of thanksgiving in the awareness that they were looking at the mighty work of God.

The Psalmist calls us to praise God for his mighty work in *Providence*. The noun "providence" comes from the verb "provide", and that is exactly what it means in the activity of God. Having created this world and having peopled it with a race of men who have human needs and problems, God did not then withdraw to a distant heaven and leave his Creation to run itself. God accepts responsibility for his Creation. He watches over his creatures, takes care of them, involves himself in their life and provides for their physical and spiritual needs.

Carved on the entrance to a science museum are words to the effect that it contains a display of the mighty works of God. The exhibits are arranged chronologically and explained according to the geological ages. First, you see the Laurentian rocks, the oldest and deepest formation known to man, and how they were inlaid by God's direction with abundant quantities of iron, the most useful of all metals. You come up to the great coal measures of the Carboniferous era and you are told how God built the mighty forests of the giant tree fern, then buried them by some awful cataclysm, storing up centuries of sunlight for the industry and comfort of mankind. In the exhibits of the Permian period you see the veins of gold, silver, copper, platinum and all the mineral wealth prepared for the coming commerce of man. In the Triassic period you see great beds of rock salt and you are told how the ancient oceans were evaporated to furnish these supplies. Another stage brings you to the great gas wells and oil wells, and you learn how through great convulsions God was storing up the light and heat and motive energy of today. The whole earth is displayed as a giant bank vault where a provident God, long before he created man, stored up the means to meet man's needs and the basic materials of our civilization. This is God's mighty work in Providence to which the Psalmist calls our attention when he summons us to praise God "*who giveth food to all flesh*".

To most people the Providence of God means something less sophisticated and more personal. You see it in a painting by Nicholas Maes, that hangs in the Rikjs Museum in Amsterdam. It shows an elderly woman in the quiet of her modest home, seated at a frugal meal of soup, fish and bread. Now she turns her thoughts to God, the giver of all gifts. Humbly and thankfully she praises him. Her work-worn hands are folded and raised in prayer, her eyes are closed, and her lips form the words of the prayer that she offers. The joys and sorrows of a long life have left their marks on her face. Its withdrawn expression reflects the intensity and the sincerity of her meditation. Not even the playful kitten tugging at the table cloth can distract her in this moment of saying grace. Around her are the signs of an ordered life in the simple furnishings of the clean room. The sturdy volume standing upright on the shelf is undoubtedly her Bible from which she has learned of God and of things eternal. A brightly polished oil lamp and an open book suggest evening hours given to reading and reflection. The artist has bathed the figure of the praying woman in a warm amber light—perhaps meant as a symbol of the light of faith within her soul, the faith that praises a provident God "*who giveth food to all flesh.*"

When the Bible speaks of God's Providence it refers not only to his work of preservation but to his work of government. The Hebrew Psalmist points to the supreme example in Israel's history. Like all the Old Testament writers he sees the history of his nation as a drama with God as the principal actor. He looks back over the succession of victories that made Israel a nation and he attributes them not to military force, not to superior strategy but to the providence of God. It was God who "*led his people through the wilderness . . . smote great kings . . . and slew famous kings . . . and gave their land for a heritage . . . even a heritage unto Israel his servant.*" To this God, this living, working, providential God, we are called to give thanks, "for his mercy endureth for ever."

Halford Luccock once told of a priceless error that appeared in the printed programme of a performance of Handel's *Messiah*. It listed the Hallelujah Chorus as follows: "The Lord God Omnipotent resigneth". Dr. Luccock asked, "Was it just an error, or was the printer a real cynic, deducing from the condition of the world that the Lord God had, in fact, resigned and had given up the world as a hopeless mess?" It might seem that way to cynics. Because *we* have lost control of our world, they make speeches and write books bemoaning that God also has lost control. It did not seem that way to the men who wrote the Bible. These men believed stubbornly that, whatever the chaos and confusion of our human situation, God still controls it. They believed that, having set history in notion. God presides over history, involves himself in history and directs history according to his wise and gracious purpose. This is God's mighty work in Providence, and the Psalmist calls us to give praise for it.

The Psalmist calls us to praise God for his mighty work in *Redemption*.

> "*O give thanks . . . To him that smote Egypt in their firstborn . . . And brought out Israel from among them . . . With a strong hand, and with a stretched out arm . . . To him which divided the Red Sea into parts . . . And made Israel to pass through the midst of it: for his mercy endureth for ever.*"

Remember that the Psalmist was writing five hundred years before the time of Christ. His Doctrine of Redemption had a different basis from ours, but its meaning was essentially the same—God had visited and redeemed his people. For centuries they had been held in captivity, chained, trapped and helpless; and what they could not do for themselves God did for them. He came to their rescue, released them from slavery and by miraculous means delivered them to freedom. This was the Psalmist's experience of God. His religion, like the religion of every faithful Israelite, took its starting-point with God's mighty work of Redemption.

In our Sunday worship we conclude the singing of the Psalms with the ancient ascription of praise, "Glory be to the Father and to the Son and to the Holy Ghost . . ." Liturgists tell us that, because the Psalms were once regarded as sub-Christian in the Church, the "Gloria" was added to make them acceptable as items of Christian worship. We might also explain this custom by saying that the addition of the "Gloria" serves to remind us that the God of the Psalmists is the God and Father of our Lord Jesus Christ. We worship this God for a far more wonderful work of Redemption—not the deliverance of one nation from slavery to another nation but the deliverance of all men from slavery to the powers of evil. We could complete the 136th Psalm, "O give thanks to him . . . who became flesh in Jesus . . . who showed us in word and deed what he is like and how he wants us to live . . . who died on the Cross to save us from sin and by his rising from the dead has opened for us the gates of eternal life . . . for his mercy endureth for ever."

How shall we grasp the total significance of God's mighty work of Redemption in Jesus Christ? Perhaps this analogy will help us to understand. Dr. Arthur Compton was one of a committee of six scientists assigned by President Roosevelt to create the first atomic bomb. In a magazine article[1] he recalls that momentous Wednesday morning, December 2, 1942, when he and the others performed their final experiment in a converted squash court in Chicago. He describes their various reactions when the experiment proved successful and they realized that a power had been liberated which would change the course of history. Relief, concern, excitement—they felt all these things. Dr. Compton says that he himself felt a sense of gratitude to God for another of his great gifts. He knew that it was a gift that put a big question mark over man's future, but about one thing there was no question, and that was that life on this earth could never be the same again after what happened on the morning of December 2, 1942. Writes Dr. Compton, "Man must now go the way of Jesus or perish."

That is exactly how the Bible writers interpret the event which we call the "Christ-Event". They see it as a mighty work of God, God's mightiest work which shook the earth and the heavens and sent its reverberations to the farthest reaches of the universe. Nothing escaped its impact. The power that was present in the birth, the ministry, the death and the Resurrection of Christ bisected the course of history. It changed everything for everybody, so that life on this earth could never be the same again. Man must now go the way of Jesus or perish. But the point is that we *can* go the way of Jesus and *not* perish. This is the new possibility that God has given to the human race and to each one of us—the choice of life instead of death. In Jesus Christ God had visited and redeemed his people.

So we have a great motive for praising God. To be sure, he has blessed us in many temporal ways beyond our deserving, and we are grateful for them, but supremely we thank him for with the Hebrew Psalmists for eternal blessings which are independent of time and circumstance. We praise God for what he is and for what he has done—for his mighty works in Creation, Providence and Redemption. "O give thanks unto the Lord; for he is good: for his mercy endureth for ever."

[1] *Guideposts*, March 1962.

all
 # 158

GOD PURSUES

"A man who has never tried to flee God has never experienced the God who is really God." So writes Paul Tillich in his influential book, *The Shaking of the Foundations*.[1] Tillich goes on to say, "There is no reason to flee from a god who is the perfect picture of everthing that is good in man . . . a god who is nothing more than a benevolent father, a father who guarantees our immortality and final happiness." But a *just* God, suggests Tillich, a God who knows everything about us, even the things that we ourselves have not the courage to face—we actually hate that God and sometimes wish he were dead. Tillich reminds us that Martin Luther was terribly shocked when he recognized within himself a hatred for the all-knowing God and a desire to escape him. Luther knew, however, that he could no more get away from God than he could get away from himself. The God whom he wanted to escape was the Ground and Depth of his own being.

Such is Tillich's masterly interpretation of the *139th Psalm*. After Tillich it seems impertinent for a grass-roots preacher to attempt an exposition of this most personal and most Christian of the Psalms. Yet I must try to expound it, because it figures so prominently among the Psalms which show the activity of God in man's experience. Besides, I have a more selfish reason. This is my favourite Psalm, one that I have long since committed to memory, the one that I often recite in my prayers as a means of approach to God. It is the Psalm that I most frequently read in my pastoral ministry, especially with people who tell me that they can no longer pray because they have lost a sense of the presence of God. I can say with Erskine of Linlathen, the great Scottish theologian and mystic, "This is the Psalm I should wish to have before me on my death-bed."

The 139th Psalm is the soliloquy of a man who has made an

[1] Penguin Books Ltd., Harmondsworth, 1964, p. 47 ff.

astounding discovery—the discovery that God knows him personally. He is more astonished than the average American would be if he suddenly found out that the President of the United States knows his name and address and telephone number. The Psalmist believes that God not only knows everything about him but that God cares for him and considers the smallest details of his life, even the purposes of his mind before they take thought-form. Indeed, the Hebrew poet is so completely overcome with a sense of God's personal interest in him that there seem to be only two people in the universe— himself and God. Out of a full heart he prays,

"O Lord, thou hast searched me, and known me. Thou knowest my downsitting and mine uprising, thou understandest my thought afar off. Thou compassest my path and my lying down, and art acquainted with all my ways. For there is not a word in my tongue, but, lo, O Lord, thou knowest it altogether. Thou hast beset me behind and before, and laid thine hand upon me."

The Psalmist does not understand how God, with a whole universe to care for, can be interested in one human being, nor does he try to understand. He has enough humility to know that man is man and God is God and that the finite mind could not grasp the infinite even if it tried. He confesses, *"Such knowledge is too wonderful for me; it is high, I cannot attain unto it."*

The writer of the 139th Psalm tells of a more wonderful discovery that he has made. He has learned from his own experience that this God who knows and cares for him is also *a God who pursues.* Forsaken by his fiancée, who refused to share his blindness, George Matheson came in his bitterness of spirit to a Cross where he found a Love that would never forsake him and he poured out his devotion by composing the deathless hymn, "O Love that wilt not let me go". This is the God whom we encounter in the 139th Psalm, a stubborn, jealous, pursuing God who loves us so much that he will not let us go. We may lose our hold upon him, but he does not lose his hold upon us. We may turn our backs on him, but he does not go away. We may run and hide from him, but he tracks us down and finds us. There is no escape from this relentless Lover of our souls. The Psalmist confesses it in prayer:

"Whither shall I go from thy spirit? or whither shall I flee from thy presence? If I ascend up into heaven, thou art there: if I make my bed in hell, behold, thou art there. If I take the wings of the morning, and dwell in the uttermost parts of the sea; even there shall thy hand lead me, and thy right hand shall hold me. If I say, Surely the darkness shall cover me; even the night shall be light about me. Yea, the darkness hideth not from thee; but the night shineth as the day: the darkness and the light are both alike to thee."

This seems to be one of life's lessons that we have to learn the hard way. Despite the Psalmist's experience and despite the experience of countless other men in the Bible and out of it, people still become fugitives from God, using the identical escape routes taken by the Psalmist and found impossible. "If I ascend up into heaven, thou art there . . ." It seems very natural for God to be in heaven and very unnatural for us to wish to ascend to heaven in order to escape him, yet that is exactly what many people do. They try to hide from God in the things of life that they describe as "heavenly", the high-flights of success and pleasure and affluence and human love which yield such a measure of personal fulfilment and happiness that they seem to make God superfluous. In the play, *J.B.*, by Archibald MacLeish, the character who impersonates Satan watches a prosperous family saying Grace at the dinner table and spits out the cynical remark, "Piety is bad enough in poor people who have to practise it. A rich man's piety stinks!" That is the popular belief—piety is a crutch for the poor, the weak, the sick, the sorrowful; a strong, healthy, happy man does not need God to support him. It is the belief of some social idealists. Make this world a heavenly place, they say, and you don't have to hope for heaven in some world-to-come. These utopians ought to be warned by Emil Brunner who pointed out as a lesson of history that, when men try to create a heaven upon earth, they often resort to coercion and violence to achieve it and end up by creating a hell instead.

There was an Old Testament prophet who told his people that God always speaks in two ways: first, he speaks in words; then, if they refuse to listen to him, he speaks in events. That suggests a reason why we cannot escape from God in the heavenly experiences of life. God gives us those experiences, and if we try to exclude him from them, they can soon take on the character of a hell. The choice is ours. We can reckon with God's mercy on the right hand or with his judgment on the left hand, we can meet him as a friend or as an enemy, we can listen to him speaking in words or we can hear his voice in events. Look at these heart-broken parents who have learned that bitter lesson. Their son has become an aimless drifter, unable to hold a steady job, a slave to the degrading habits that will one day ruin him. Their daughter's marriage has collapsed, and people whisper about her immoral conduct. From both children the parents have received nothing but ingratitude and disappointment and they cannot understand the reason for it, because theirs was such a happy home, a place of love and warmth and security, a heaven upon earth. They gave their children everything, everything but a sense of gratitude and obedience to God who was the author of their happiness. They thought that they didn't need God; they excluded him from their earthly heaven; and, having refused to reckon with God in heaven, they now have to reckon with him in hell.

Some people purposely go to hell in the effort to escape from God. They sell their souls to the Devil and make his house their home, certain that there at least God will never track them down. They have the idea that, if they can just sink deep enough into the slime of irreligion and immorality, they will put themselves beneath the reach of God's loving concern. God will no longer be interested in them. It is a mistaken idea, as the Psalmist realized when he confessed to God, ". . . if I make my bed in hell, behold, thou art there."

Inevitably we recall Francis Thompson's immortal ode, "The Hound of Heaven", a poem which is really a modern version of the 139th Psalm, because the experience of the poet runs parallel to that of the Psalmist. Thompson was a fugitive from God. As a youth, brought up in a religious home, he studied for the priesthood, then for medicine, each time failing through his own laziness and lack of interest. Nothing seems to have come out of his early years except a love of narcotics which all but destroyed him. As a young man he lost himself in London, picking up odd jobs, blacking boots, selling matches, holding horses, anything for a few pennies that would buy him what we call a "fix". The only decent thing left in his life was a love of poetry. He wrote a few poems and on an impulse sent some of them to Wilfred Meynell, an editor and publisher, who saw signs of genius in them. Meynell and his gifted wife searched out the poet and drew him from his pitiable surroundings. This is how they described his appearance: "No such figure had been looked for; more ragged and unkempt than the average beggar, with no shirt beneath his coat, and bare feet in broken shoes." From that wretched condition Thompson was rescued for English literature and for the enrichment of the world by two people in whom he recognized the love of God. He came to realize that, even though he had made his bed in the hell of misery and the darkness of despair, even though he had secluded himself from men and fled to the uttermost bounds of loneliness, yet he could not escape the pursuing love of God. Read his heart's testimony:

"I fled Him, down the nights and down the days;
I fled Him, down the arches of the years;
I fled Him, down the labrinthine ways
Of my own mind; and in the midst of tears
I hid from Him, and under running laughter.
Up vistaed hopes I sped;
And shot, precipitated
Adown Titanic glooms of chasmèd fears,
From those strong Feet that followed, followed after.
But with unhurrying chase,
And unperturbèd pace,
Deliberate speed, majestic instancy
They beat—and a Voice beat
More instant than the Feet—
'All things betray thee, who betrayest Me'."[1]

If the farthest limits of emotion cannot provide a refuge from God, neither can the farthest limits of space. "If I take the wings of the morning . . ." prayed the Psalmist; and that image has suddenly assumed a literal meaning in our technical civilization when jet aeroplanes circle the earth and cosmonauts cruise among the stars. Some people suppose that by taking the wings of the morning we have actually escaped God; they

[1] Published in *The World's Great Religious Poetry*, compiled by Caroline Miles Hill (New York, The Macmillan Company, 1938), p. 45.

suppose that every time a space-man goes up, God comes down. A few years ago Prime Minister Khrushchev of Russia gave an interview to C. L. Sulzberger of the *New York Times* in which he said mockingly, "As to Paradise, we have heard a lot about it from the priests. So we decided to find out for ourselves. First, we sent up our explorer Yuri Gagarin. He circled the globe and found nothing in outer space. It's pitch dark there, he said; no Garden of Eden, nothing like Heaven. So we decided to send another explorer. We sent Gherman Titov and told him to fly for a whole day. After all, Gagarin was up there only an hour and a half. So he might have missed Paradise. We told him to take a good look. Well, he took off, came back and confirmed Gagarin's conclusion. He reported that there was nothing there."[1]

The speaker in this case happened to be a Russian communist, but there is nothing peculiarly nationalistic or doctrinaire about his point of view. Many people of differing ideologies in all countries firmly believe that, now that man has literally taken the wings of the morning and travelled to outer space, he has left God behind with all the other myths of his earthbound existence. Man has come of age, he has outdistanced God, he has emigrated to new continents of thought and achievement where God will never find him. That is one point of view, but there are other people, including some reputable scientists, who hold a diametrically opposite viewpoint. They believe that, if the modern explorer opened his eyes when he reached these new continents of thought and achievement, he would discover that God is there ahead of him, a greater and more magnificent God then he ever knew before. He might discover that he has, in fact, left behind his own puny ideas of God and that now for the first time in his life he is coming close to God himself. This real God does not dwell in outer space. He contains outer space. Outer space is one of the many mansions in his house. This God contains us. In him we live and move and have our being and we shall never escape him until we cease to be.

There are many ways of interpreting the final friend of all fugitives—"If I say, Surely the darkness shall cover me; even the night shall be light about me . . ." It could mean the darkness of death—which explains why the Church has traditionally included a reading of the 139th Psalm in the Burial Service for

[1] *The Christian Century*, December 6, 1961, p. 1456.

the victims of suicide. A distraught girl telephoned me recently. She refused to identify herself. 'I am going to commit suicide," she said. "I have made plans to make it look like an accident. Only one thing is holding me back, and I want you to give me an honest answer: Will I have to face God after I am dead?" I begged her to read the 139th Psalm. Or it could mean the darkness of agnosticism, because that's what agnosticism very often is—an attempt to escape intellectually the God whom we have not the courage to face in real life. Just close your mind, take a deep breath and tell yourself that God doesn't exist. You can close your eyes and pretend that the light doesn't exist too. Both gestures are equally futile, as the Psalmist confessed to God, "Yea, the darkness hideth not from thee; but the night shineth as the day: the darkness and the light are both alike to thee."

One of the most searching and starkly frank pieces of autobiography ever published is a book called *The Towers of Trebizond*. The author, Rose Macaulay, tells of standing at the rail of a cruise ship on the Black Sea overlooking the Turkish port of Trebizond. It was a Sunday morning, and the other members of the party had attended Anglican Mass, but she did not join them, because she was having an affair with another woman's husband and she had made this journey to get away from God, not to confront him. Suddenly she heard behind her the voice of the Anglican priest, "How much longer are you going on like this, shutting the door against God?" "I don't know," she replied weakly. The priest looked at her sternly and said, "I hope, I pray, that you will know before it is too late." She stood there, alone again, looking at the church towers in the distance, thinking of the alternating struggle in her life between the Church and agnosticism, admitting to herself that agnosticism had never been more than a refuge from God. She remembered that she was an agnostic through school and university, then, at twenty-three, took up with the Church again; but the Church met its Waterloo a few years later when she took up with adultery, and this adultery lasted on and on, and she was still in it now and she saw no prospect of its ending except with death—the death of one of three people, and perhaps it would be her own. (That was how the story did end—with a car accident that injured her and killed the man she loved.) Now, in this moment of moral honesty, she admitted to herself that agnosticism "seemed the only refuge, since taking the wings of the morning and fleeing to the uttermost parts of the sea is said to provide no hope, only another confrontation."[1]

Surely you can see that the 139th is the most intensely personal of all the Psalms. Can anyone read it without suspecting that the Psalmist's experience mirrors his own? Much of our life is an attempt, down the avenues of heaven and hell and new knowledge and agnosticism, to escape this God who knows us better than we know ourselves, but we cannot escape him for the very reason that he has known us since before we were born. So prays the Psalmist: "*For thou hast possessed my reins: thou hast covered me in my mother's womb.*" This all-knowing God is not to be cursed but praised: "*I will praise thee; for I am fearfully and wonderfully made: marvellous are thy works; and that my soul knoweth right well.*"

But why should we want to escape God? Does he not bring blessing in his hand? The God of man's experience is not like Police Inspector Javert, tracking down the escaped convict, pursuing him through the sewers of Paris, so that he can arrest the man and lock him up in a prison cell and chain him to the wall. Our God is like a shepherd who leaves the rest of his flock while he goes searching for a single stray and, when he finds the lost sheep, he cradles it tenderly in his arms and brings it back to the warmth and safety of the fold. Our God is like a father who does not wait for the return of a prodigal son but follows the rebellious boy into the far country because he loves him and wants him to come home and be the child of his love again. Our God brings us not accusation but forgiveness, not imprisonment but freedom, not death but life—and this because he loves us with a greater love than we can ever imagine. In his prayer the Psalmist awakens to this love: "*How precious also are thy thoughts unto me, O God! how great is the sum of them! If I should count them, they are more in number than the sand: when I awake, I am still with thee*".

The 139th is not only the most personal, it is the most Christian of the Psalms. It was inevitable that this pursuing God, who knows us better than we know ourselves, should at a point in history thrust himself into our human situation

[1] Rose Macaulay, *The Towers of Trebizond* (Collins Fontana Books, London & Glasgow, 1962), pp. 54–6.

and come where we are, loving us even when we hound him to a terrible death, and still loving until he breaks down all barriers and wins our final allegiance. The God of the Psalmist is the God who cries to us from a Cross: "You can do with me what you like; you can break my bones and drain my blood and bruise my flesh but you cannot stop me from being what I am, the Father who loves you and will not let you go."

GOD ACTS

There is a delightful story about a man who went to an old friend to ask for a loan of money without collateral and at no interest. The friend assumed at once that deadpan expression and evasive eye that we mortals use when discussing finances. He replied that he frankly did not feel their present friendship close enough to justify such a claim on it. That jolted the supplicant. "John," he exlaimed, "how can you say that to me? We were boys together. I coached you for examinations. I saved you from drowning once. I helped you get started in business. I persuaded my cousin to marry your sister." "Oh," replied John, with an inclusive wave of his hand, "I remember all that. What bothers me is—what have you done for me lately?"

That question bothers a lot of people about God. What has God done for us lately? What is he doing for us right now? We remember that God has done some great things in the past. With the Psalmists of the Old Testament we praise him for his mighty works in Creation, Providence and Redemption. But these are God's finished works; they were finished long before we were born. We want to know what God has done for us lately and what, if anything, he is doing for us right now.

Psalm 147 is one of the greatest statements in the Bible of the activity of God. It opens with a call to thanksgiving: *"Praise ye the Lord: for it is good to sing praises unto our God; for it is pleasant; and praise is comely."* Every verse begins with a verb, twenty-six of them in all, each setting forth some phase of God's activity. We are told that God *heareth, telleth, lifteth, maketh, goeth, delighteth, sendeth, causeth,* etc. These verbs are all in the present tense, as compared to those Psalms which praise God for his mighty works in the past and are therefore set in the past tense. The 147th Psalm shows him as a God who has not only done great things but who does great things. He does them for Israel, but the point is that he does them. He is *a God who acts.* A study of this Psalm may help us to answer the question, What has God done for us lately and what, if anything, is he doing for us right now? Let us consider some of the general truths which it teaches us about God.

Psalm 147 teaches that the God who created all nature provides for the needs of the individual. He who "*telleth the number of the stars*" is also he who "*healeth the broken in heart, and bindeth up their wounds.*" The God "*who covereth the heaven with clouds*" is also he who "*giveth to the beast his food, and to the young ravens which cry.*" This God is worthy of our praise. So declares the Psalmist: "*Sing unto the Lord with thanksgivigg; sing praise upon the harp unto our God.*"

Jesus came to tell us about such a God and make him known to us. The Teacher of Galilee used many figures of speech to convince people of God's personal concern for them. He said, "The very hairs of your head are all numbered . . . ye are of more value than many sparrows." The most precious picture of God in Jesus' teaching and in all the Bible imagery is that of the Shepherd caring for his sheep, a picture which became more meaningful to me on a day when my family and I climbed Mount Snowdon in North Wales. It was springtime, and the streams were swollen. On the opposite bank of one of them we suddenly saw a new-born lamb huddled helplessly in a hollow of ground. The girls and I remained there while my wife walked further up the mountain to a farm house. After a while she returned with the farmer who tenderly and joyously picked up the animal and cradled it in his arm as if it were a human baby. In his lilting Welsh voice he thanked us and said, "I have been looking for this lamb for two days". Such is the Bible picture of God—a Shepherd who leaves the rest of his flock while he searches for a single stray, a God willing to let Creation run itself while he looks to the welfare of the least of his creatures.

This is not an easy truth to believe about God. It raises the old problem of Providence-in-General versus Providence-in-Particular. Many people, who concede that God may be actively concerned about his whole Creation, nevertheless ask, How can a great God possibly be concerned about the least of his creatures? The answer is—because he is God. That is what makes him God, and that is what makes him great. The Psalmist acknowledges it; "*Great is our Lord, and of great power: his understanding is infinite.*"

Stepping on the bus, a child turned instinctively as she heard her name called, "Hello Margaret". For a moment the child stood spellbound, because the greeting came from the Principal of her school who smiled and walked on. That night the little girl said wonderingly to her parents, "We have five hundred pupils in our school. I've never spoken to the Principal before. I didn't know that she knew me. Yet she called me by name". Exactly! It explains why the woman was an admired and beloved Principal. She made it her business to know and call each of her pupils by name. That is what makes God worthy of our praise and love. In his almighty Providence not a single person is lost. He knows and cares for each as though he cared for that one alone.

Moreover, God's concern for his creatures is an active concern, as the Psalmist knew from his own experience. There are many people like this Hebrew poet who can say that, when they have opened the doors of their lives to God, he has entered and acted and done for them what they could never do for themselves. Such was the radiant witness of James Davidson Ross whose beloved wife, Clare, died in middle-age after a long illness. In a tender book, that bears her name as the title, he tells how the years of crisis brought them face to face with God:

"It was a time in which all our values and beliefs were turned upside down, all our self-sufficiency, pretensions, and faith in our own ability to judge and deal with any situation— the whole façade of humbug to which so many of us cling went overboard. We came face to face with a situation that was utterly beyond our control, in which we were helpless; and at the bottom of a very black well of despair we discovered that the God we had ignored or rejected all our lives was real, living, and *there*." Reminding us of all that is written these days about the so-called "image of God", Mr. Ross goes on to say, "I have no image of God, but, through the teaching of the living Christ, I have got a love for him as that which I could have for a well-loved father. For this unthinkable God who, as great minds from St. Paul to Tillich have so rightly comprehended him, is the root and ground and depth of our whole being, is still the same Father who knows, cares, and—if we make one slightest move toward him—acts!"[1]

[1] *Op. cit.*, pp. 79–80.

The doubter may still feel constrained to ask, "But what has God done for *me* lately?" There can be only one answer: God may have done more for you than you imagine, if your life has really been open to him. Jacob, fleeing from his brother, Esau, came by night to a lonely place in the wilderness where he slept and saw in his dream a ladder ascending from earth to heaven. In the morning, when he awakened, he said, "Surely the Lord is in this place, and I did not know it." Have you never even felt the least constraint to say the same thing? Have you never thought that the forces which have been brought to bear on your life in recent months, the forces that befriended, protected, guided and chastened you, may in fact, be the unperceived and undeserved activity of God? *Daddy Long Legs* is the story of a girl in an orphanage who was befriended by an unknown benefactor. Through her childhood and youth he acted constantly for her welfare, but always keeping his identity a secret. Though she often met him she did not know him as her benefactor. She thought of him only as a shadow that she had once seen cast from an open office door. It is a picture of people whose lives have been nurtured, whose mistakes have been buttressed and whose achievements have been shaped by Someone in the shadows who has no name to them. The Lord has been present and active in their lives, and they did not know it. This is what God has done for us lately. This is how he acts.

The 147th Psalm teaches that the God who ordained all law administers his laws. This is the thought suggested in verse six, "*The Lord lifteth up the meek: he casteth the wicked down to the ground*"; and again in verse eleven, "*The Lord taketh pleasure in them that fear him, in those that hope in his mercy.*" The God of the Psalmist's experience is not neutral. He is not indifferent to the way that men behave. This God has purposes and preferences. He takes pleasure in those who obey his laws and he is displeased with those who disobey them. Therefore he acts. He involves himself in human life, breaking down evil and building up good.

Again it raises the problem of Providence-in-Particular, a problem that perplexes many people. Once when I went to visit a man in serious trouble I asked if he would like me to pray with him. "No", he replied honestly, "It would take a miracle to get me out of this mess, and I never pray for miracles. I don't believe that even God can break his own laws."

It is a rational and stalwart point of view but surely it assumes that we know all there is to know about the laws of God. It takes for granted that the last word on nature's laws has been spoken—which is demonstrably not true, because we are continually discovering new laws which were unknown to previous generations. Many years ago a Dutch ambassador, describing his native country, told the King of Siam that during the winter the water became so hard that men could actually walk on it. The king flew into a rage. He was not prepared, he said, to believe anything so ridiculous, preposterous and impossible. How would that autocratic little monarch have reacted if the ambassador had predicted televison and satellites and jet aeroplanes and space travel? He would probably have chopped off His Excellency's head. It is never within our competence to decide what is possible or impossible within the laws of nature; and if we cannot fix limits on man's achievements, how can we fix them on God's? What we call miracles may not be miracles at all but the activity of God operating according to his own laws on a higher scale than any with which we are familiar.

If we have decided that God has to be bound by his own laws, it means that we accord God less moral freedom than we allow ourselves. To an extent, a magistrate is bound by laws but he still retains the right to administer those laws for the well-being of the offender and society. If this were not so, every murderer would have to be hanged, and the child of a broken home would receive exactly the same sentence as a hardened criminal. Jesus specifically promised that we can expect greater generosity from God than from a human magistrate. Why? Because God loves us and because people are more important to him than laws. In his view Nature is not a computer governed by impersonal, immutable law; it is a monarchy governed by a personal Sovereign who, having ordained its laws in the first place, reserves the right to administer those laws, to modify, change or waive them, if necessary, for the well-being of the subjects whom he loves.

If this is a true picture of God in man's experience it gives all the more point to our question: What has God done for us lately and what, if anything, is he doing right now? To some people God appears to be doing nothing. They ask, If God is really a God who acts, who has purposes and preferences, who takes pleasure in those who obey him and displeasure in those who disobey him, so that he breaks down evil and builds up good, why does he not intervene in our muddled human situation and take a hand in setting it right? Surely these people have too limited an idea of God's activity which the Bible sees not only in terms of intervention but in terms of involvement. God is not only an external factor whom we bring to bear on our human situation from the outside; he is an internal factor already at work within our human situation, and it is our business to recognize him and discover what he is doing and co-operate with his purposes. The very tragedies that we deplore— the revolutions, the wars, the tyrannies, the hunger and the senseless slaughter that seem to make mockery of an active God—may, if we view them in the light of God's righteous judgment, become sure signs of God's activity.

Before complaining about the inactivity of God in our human situation, let us make certain that we look at that situation in its wholeness. Do we see nothing but moral chaos and suffering? Do we not see other factors which convince us that God or someone like God is doing marvellous things in the world today? The heroism and devotion of Christian missionaries in hostile countries; the relief of human suffering now being administered on a tremendous scale by great national and inter-national social agencies; the protest against racial and religious bigotry being offered by people who are able to think straightly and feel humanely; the championship of intellectual freedom and civil liberties by distinguished scientists, courageous educa-tors and enlightened churchmen and laymen; the fresh, valiant, creative thinking which has been done and is being done with respect to the abolition of poverty and war—this is what God has done for us lately; this is how he acts.

Psalm 147 teaches that the God who governs all nations calls out one particular nation. The theme of the whole Psalm is God's solicitude for his people Israel. What God does he does for Israel. So concludes the Psalm: "*He sheweth his word unto Jacob, his statutes and his judgments unto Israel. He hath not dealt so with any nation: and as for his judgments, they have not known them. Praise ye the Lord.*" This was indeed the God of the Psalmist's experience, precisely because he belonged to the nation Israel. To the Hebrew poet God's activity was not theory but fact. He knew it to be historically true that the God of the whole earth had called out one nation to be his covenant people and that to them he had given his words, his statutes and his judgments, dealing with them as he dealt with no other nation.

As Christians we believe that what was once true for Israel is now true for the Church. We believe that the Church is the spiritual successor to Israel, God's new covenant people, constituted not on the basis of racial solidarity but on the basis of faith in Jesus Christ and obedience to him. This new people God calls out from all the peoples of the earth, entrusts them with his Gospel and deals with them as with no other human society. We do not presume that the Church has a monopoly on God's activity but we do believe that God's solicitude for his Church is a truth that needs to be doubly stressed in these days when some of our more radical thinkers have thrown up a false dichotomy between the Church and the world. They would go so far as to say that God has deserted the Church, at least the institutional Church, and has transferred his activity to schools and hospitals and labour unions and theatres and political parties and other structures of secular society. Does this explain, perhaps, why the enrollment in our theological colleges has sunk to an alarmingly low level? Does it explain why middle-aged men are leaving the parish ministry to take jobs as teachers and social workers and television producers? Most of them feel no sense of disloyalty. They still see themselves as servants of God but they believe that God is now more active in the world than in the Church and they want to be in the mainstream of God's activity.

We must respect their decision, because every man has to work out his own salvation, but we must also ask whether they are correct in assuming that God has ceased to be active in the life of his Church? The Church exists, and that alone is a sign of God's activity, because if ever an institution has died a thousand deaths, that institution is the Church. Cynics who draw pictures of the Church as a sinking ship have no originality. The Church has been a sinking ship for centuries, and the miracle of it is that it remains afloat and continues to pick up survivors from other ships. The World Council of Churches has a symbol—a small boat tossed about on a furious ocean. The boat contains a Cross, and therein lies the secret of its remaining afloat. One factor keeps the Church from being smashed to bits—the indwelling presence of the Crucified and Risen Christ. He, the Son of God, started the Church on its perilous voyage through time; and the Church survives only because he, the love of God in action, involves himself in its life.

No one will deny that the Spirit of God is mightily active in the world today, far beyond the borders of organized Christianity. But those who take this as evidence that God has ceased to be active within his Church have not come to terms with certain facts. Here is one fact: In a single twelve-month period the World Council of Churches distributed some twenty-six thousand tons of food, clothing and medical supplies; established new homes for more than nineteen thousand refugees; sent one and a half million dollars in cash for emergency help to victims of floods, earthquakes, fires and famine; and provided more than six million dollars for inter-Church and inter-Mission Aid projects throughout the world—all this assistance with no political or ecclesiastical strings attached. Here is another fact: In Rhodesia the only agency which today provides secondary school education for African students is the Church; and this can be equalled in other developing countries where the Church is still the major source of healing, enlightenment and social service. Still another fact: In Formosa the number of churches in one major denomination has been doubled during the past ten years; and in Russia the number of Christians who received Communion last Easter exceeded the number in Britain. One more fact: In a village in Alaska, where the Church was the last of the social amenities to be provided, a sophisticated woman said to the minister through an alcoholic breath, "You know, Reverend, no one seemed to give a damn for us until the Church came."

How shall we explain that, despite all its stuffiness, its slowness and its weakness, the institutional Church continues not only to survive but to function effectively as the most healing, hopeful, charitable, reconciling, character-building force in the world today? There is no explanation except that God still cares for his Church, still singles it out, uses it, works through it, strengthens it and deals with it as he deals with no other human society. This is what God has done for us lately. This is how "Praise ye the Lord."